W9-AAI-394

E L E A N O R ' S   R E B E L L I O N

ELEANOR'S REBELLION

A Mother, Her Son, and Her Secret

DAVID SIFF

 Alfred A. Knopf New York 2000

This Is a Borzoi Book, Published by Alfred A. Knopf

Copyright © 2000 by David Siff

All rights reserved under International and Pan-American Copyright Conventions. Published
in the United States by Alfred A. Knopf, a division of Random House, Inc., New York, and
simultaneously in Canada by Random House of Canada Limited, Toronto. Distributed by
Random House, Inc., New York.

www.aaknopf.com

Knopf, Borzoi Books, and the colophon are registered trademarks of Random House, Inc.

Library of Congress Cataloging-in-Publication Data
Siff, David.
Eleanor's rebellion : a mother, her son, and her secret / David Siff. — 1st ed.
p.   cm.
ISBN 0-375-40175-X
1. Siff, David   2. Siff, Eleanor.   3. Adoptees—United States—Biography.
4. Mothers—United States—Biography.   5. Adoption—United States—Case studies.
6. Birthfathers—United States—Identification—Case studies.   7. Heflin, Van,
1910–1971.   I. Title.
HV874.82.S53 A3 2000
362.73'4'092—dc21   [B]   99-058952

Manufactured in the United States of America
First Edition

To the memory of Eleanor Segal Siff

Where's her death? Do you have time to find

that subject before your song burns up?

Where does she drain out of me? . . . a girl, almost . . .

— R I L K E , *Sonnets to Orpheus*

My mother, about age sixteen

PART ONE

A Woman Rebels

*P*amela Thistlewaite does not take to flouncy gowns and whale-bone corsets well. She is long and rangy, her body is far more comfortable in the free play of riding clothes: tapered trousers tucked into English boots with their perfect silver spurs. She moves with her wits about her; nothing is more apparent than that the force which powers her comes from clear-eyed intelligence rather than from the fluid way hip is joined to thigh. She is simply not the girl Judge Thistlewaite planned for, though adoring he is . . . and helpless *before the irrepressible force of her very winning and unpredictable personality.*

She is courted by the long-suffering, decent Thomas Lane, whose ardor is, to her, unfortunately inert. She is, at least for the moment, set aflame by a volatile ne'er-do-well named Gerald. We know Gerald from hundreds of old melodramas. He is young, penniless, full of imagination and ambition. But it is his heart we will forever mistrust. Whether he's an artist, a criminal, or a weakling, he's just plain trouble. He caresses dreams that go off like Roman candles, leaving everything dark afterward. It is the peculiar irony of dramas such as these that Pamela's choice of him as a lover is immediately forgivable whereas his choice of her is not. The man is married but says nothing about this to poor Pamela.

From this union a child is conceived and a two-hour plot delivered. The bounder does not stay with the heroine. The heroine gives birth and courageously decides, against the dictates of convention and common sense, to raise and take care of the child herself. Her lover never sees his daughter and, in fact, remains unaware of her existence until she is fully grown. We are not made privy to his state of mind. From the moment she conceived, it is Pamela's misfortune that pulls at our heartstrings. Heroically, she goes on alone, the epitome of an independent woman until, after many years, she finally allows herself to submit to the faithful ministrations of Thomas Lane, whom she marries and comes to love.

A Woman Rebels
RKO, 1936 (87 minutes)

ONE

1.

Nineteen seventy-five. I'm standing on another line. It's a clear winter day and the cold is still on my hands and face. The bare green walls and dirty marble floor, the clerks sitting behind cages, the people filing through the room, all of it triggers vague fantasies of Ellis Island at the turn of the century, when grandparents, brothers, sisters, aunts, uncles, and cousins arrived one after another. Today, I'm glad to be in out of the cold, dreaming. This corner of lower Manhattan gets winds that take you like grappling hooks. There were once ponds below the streets and office buildings, ponds where holes were broken in the ice and Indians fished, huddled next to small fires.

I can't really figure out why I've let myself in for this. I'm reluctant to call this free will. I am utterly devoid of belief that I'll find my birth time. But it's become an obsession—for an astrology chart, of all things—like finding land must have been for Erik the Red. It's been two weeks since I was here last to get the birth certificate that *didn't* contain the information I was looking for. I've taken the document out of my pocket countless times and read down the grained yellow page, line by line, name, mother's name, father's name, date of birth, place of birth, hospital, attending physician, and so on. Nothing. There are 1,440 minutes in twenty-four hours. One of those minutes on September 28, 1935, is mine alone. I share September 28 with Ed Sullivan and Brigitte Bardot, but which of those 1,440 minutes with its precise subdivision of seconds belongs to me? That is the question, that's why I'm stamping on my ice-cold feet waiting in line. None of my relatives had the answer. I've tried to run down the records of a hospital that's gone out of business, of doctors dead, missing, or jailed. *I've been here before, why am I back?* I'm forty, the war is over, South Vietnam has surrendered, the NLF has won. It's become weird out there. A little bird named Squeaky Fromme has gotten it into her spooned-out patriotic mind to shoot Gerald Ford. All right, my hair is down to here, I smoke, drop tabs, teach Tolstoy and Carlos Casteneda to cops, but I'm like a dog with a bone: I can't let go of the idea that a sea drop of life can be revealed in the mystic round of an astrology wheel.

The line moves slowly toward the clerk in the cage. I think of my father. He died a couple of months ago, but I'm thinking of him now because I remember an Ellis Island story of his about Uncle George getting us our family name—Siff (as in Syph)—the name that launched a hundred bloody noses, scraped knees, and childhood ambuscades through three generations. It was an anonymous clerk who came up with the name, some worn-out, underpaid, red-nosed, angry clock-puncher who loved jokes and hated his work. "Name?" "Ziev. Ygor Ziev." A look, three strokes of a pen, and an official stamp. "Welcome to America, George Siff." For about five years, until he began to understand English, George Siff thought his name sounded better, softer, in translation.

I have my spiel ready when my turn comes. I hold the yellow paper up and jab at it, emphasizing to the clerk how important it is to get an accurate birth time. She explains that birth times weren't always recorded back then. She can't understand why I'm fishing through the ice. I tell her I want to know about all records pertaining to my birth that may be on file at this office. The clerk asks to see the document. I give it to her and watch her peruse it. A pause, a hiatus, something. The clerk suddenly holds the paper up, pokes a finger at it, and barks: "Who gave this to you? You had no business getting this!"

I have no idea what she means—maybe she's telling me I goofed in applying for a certificate that didn't have a birth time on it as opposed to another that does. I take the paper from her to see what it is she's trying to tell me. I look at the title. Where's the mistake? The words across the top, in large black Gothic letters are perfectly clear:

CERTIFICATE OF BIRTH

Then, suddenly, I see it. In all the times I've read and reread this document, folding it, putting it away, taking it out, reading it over line by line again and again, I've somehow missed it every time. Two small words like a name in the phone book, in plain roman print, fly up at me like a bat out of a barn door:

By Adoption

But I have no real memory of this moment. I have a picture in my mind, but going past the frozen frame of it is a little like going to the door, sticking out a hand, trying to feel the night. I have language—and a story—twenty-two years after the fact, but in that moment, as in the afterflash of the snapshot, there is only a negative, a face with glasses. Was the person black or white, in light-colored clothing or dark? Impossible to say. I know I held on to the document, because I still have it. But I don't remember how I got out of the room and down into the street. All I can remember is the feeling of flight, shrinking away from the interior of the Municipal Building as though from light or a cross. I remember that there was a bloodshot sunset filled with a royal canopy of dark clouds; the image is a feeling—a sensation of flying, of somehow lifting off the ground over rooftops, neighborhoods, interfering with flight patterns from Newark and Long Island, slashing through radio signals, satellite transmissions, waves of background static, over to the West Side, up Sixth Avenue to 13th Street, all the way to my mother's door.

It is as though she has been waiting for this moment for years. She does not betray a flicker of surprise. "Oh, *that*," she says, looking at the certificate as though it were an overlooked parking ticket. She is a small woman, young-looking for sixty. But in her red robe she looks a little like a potted plant in the middle of her green, plumped sofa. With her head bowed, her perfectly done hair riding above her head like a sail, her glasses hanging on her nose, she is gathering herself. When she raises her head, her brown eyes are clear. "This is not what you think," she says. Her tone is light, full of irony, there is no weight at all to the history she is carrying. She explains that I am hers and my father's but that they had me out of wedlock when they were too poor to get married. That's it. They got married a couple of years later, adopted me after that to protect my legal rights.

"You *know* your father," she explains.

I think I do. I know that I look exactly like my mother and that my father's thinking is as clear to me as her features. I know my parents. What I don't know is that the feeling of disappointment I have in the pit of my stomach is part of my blindness, like missing the words on that birth certificate. It makes me move like a sleepwalker, someone with different energy. I am unaware of it but I am stepping out of the snapshot into the darkness, moving with my hands out.

I tell myself I'm still looking for my birth time, this I must have. I think I know where I can find it now, one last chance: the adoption record itself. That's fine, my mother says, as though she's just gotten her nails and hair done and is looking forward to dinner and an evening at Lincoln Center.

Adoption records are sealed permanently in the vast majority of the fifty states. I have my mother's blessing, but that is beside the point, the law is the law. The person who tells me this is an elderly Irish clerk at Surrogate's Court, but he does not simply send me away. He tells me I can petition the court if I wish, and maybe a judge will let me see the part of it I want, my birth time. I go ahead.

Months go by. I submit draft after draft of this petition, which the clerk looks at and corrects for me. In this time we become, if not friends, familiar with each other. He calls me Ace, as though I'm a friend of his son's or someone he occasionally runs into at Gaelic football games. I think of him as one of the old guys in Inwood Park, down by the rocks, who, when I was a kid, used to tell me stories about shad runs in the Hudson and finding arrowheads in the caves up in the hills. But, nearly three decades later, I suspect that all along I was, to him, with my long hair and dreams of Revelation Through Astrology, someone he was trying to coax back across the divide between generations. "In those days, having a kid when you weren't married, Ace, especially among immigrant families, that was a big deal—not like it is now—you should always keep that in mind," he told me. Finally, one day, he took me aside and sat me down on a plain black bench in the hallway outside his office.

"Ace, I'm sorry to tell you this, but I took the liberty of looking at your record, and the gentleman you thought was your father isn't your father," he said. The clerk was a long, thin man, bony but very straight. When he sat or moved it seemed as if it was in segments, like parts of a drawbridge. He sat next to me on the bench, the platform of his knees, the pillars of his legs, the stanchion of his torso, pulleys and levers of arms and hands, the tower of his head all working in harness to raise the barrier between one side of the water and the other. He explained that by law he wasn't allowed to tell me what he had seen, but that I should keep in mind I was adopted in 1941, a few months after my brother was born. He told me to be kind to my mother.

I did not hear him.

My mother is waiting for me on a day in early spring. I have come to her weekend home upstate. It is a sanctuary, a place nestled at the bottom of a long swell of land, all green now, closed in by hills and bordered by long, open fields. I can see her on this windblown April day as she walks with me, away from the house, along the edge of a large pond. The sail of her hair in the wind is ragged. She's turned up the collar of her purple wool spring jacket; she's wearing a fashionable white sweater and a pair of tapered tan slacks. She's a little too elegant in this setting but nonetheless possesses the alertness and stride of a sportswoman, not someone whose masts are torn, whose hull is being blown across an angry sea.

We sit on a double-swing redwood bench, facing each other. The swing moves slowly back and forth as we talk. There are willows ringing the pond, brilliant bright-green curtains reaching down to the water's edge. My mother listens. Her face has the same clear-eyed expression it had when this first came up months ago. The only hint of what she may be feeling is in a mad attempt she makes to light a cigarette against the wind. This takes place when I am trying to explain to her what I have learned. I am forced to stop as again and again she sparks a lighter that flares and blows out, until, twisted halfway in the seat, covering her face with the mask of her hands like the Hunchback of Notre Dame, she finally lights up, raises her chin, and blows off a huge cloud of blue smoke that whips back into her face and hair.

At last I finish my story. I emphasize to her the timing of the adoption. My mother is someone who lives on the edges of exaggeration and drama—just as I do. I highlight the timing business by telling her that there was something in the record about Dad's actually wanting to protect me legally after the birth of his first *biological* child. My mother stares at me when I use this expression. I have no idea what she is thinking. At that moment, my uncle Morty is hauling a bag of trash across the lawn to a barrel at the edge of a field. He distracts me like a hawk in the sky, so that I am almost surprised when I hear my mother's reply.

"Oh, what the hell," she says, the words almost barking out of her, "of course you know who your father is!"

I stare at her. She is glaring at me. For one crazy moment, all I can think of is my uncle with his bag of garbage.

"No," I say, "I don't."

"Your father is Van Heflin!" she says.

I don't remember then what I said—or felt. I know that the next day, or maybe later that afternoon, and then for a long time afterward, whenever I told the story, I insisted on making a joke out of it.

"Better Van Heflin than Van Johnson," I said I said.

But I know I never did. This story, more than twenty years later, is still moving out from a center that was as frozen in that moment as the tundra. What I have learned since is that neither my heart nor my mother's was buried there, but I still cannot recover the moment, only what came after, the next day, the years since, and slowly, and only by degrees, in the way that heat moves through an immense plain of ice.

2.

Nineteen thirty-five. My mother, Eleanor Segal, nineteen, discovered she was pregnant with me in her fourth month. Until then she had been having partial periods and was free of morning sickness. She lived at home with her parents and two sisters in a comfortable but cramped apartment on the Grand Concourse in the Bronx, near 163rd Street.

She grew to suspect she might be pregnant because she couldn't account for why she was gaining weight yet eating less and less. She was also moodier than usual. Her sister Harriet, four years older, had recently graduated from college and become a social worker. Harriet was the responsible one of the three sisters. She was bossy, always trying to correct her sisters while resenting the burden it placed on her. My mother normally shrugged this off. But these days anything her sister said annoyed her. If Harriet asked whether she had taken their ill and slightly retarded sister, Nancy, out that day, my mother would tell her to mind her own business. If Harriet asked whether my mother had been downtown or who she had seen that day, my mother got up and left the table.

My mother needed to see a doctor and knew only one, an uncle named Jacob, who was a tuberculosis specialist. When she was sixteen, this uncle had tried to force himself on her. I never learned whether he had succeeded.

Now she set out to see him again. If I close my eyes and try to imagine her from family photographs, I can almost see what she was wearing as she made the trip up the Concourse to her uncle's office: a long, plain dark dress that buttoned straight up to her throat and had a prim white collar with a needlework design of geometric figures, white on white, against the navy-blue material of the dress. She wears dark stockings and lace-up boots, no jewelry, carries no handbag, wears no gloves—and, this day especially, is without makeup. Her thick, wavy hair is pulled back and woven into a tight bun that is secured by a network of invisible pins and a small tortoiseshell comb.

It was a day in mid-spring, in the same neighborhood where I grew up. Stepping out of the house, if the weather was clear, you couldn't help noticing flower beds in backyards and in window boxes, the surprise of a garden or a rosebush in a vacant lot. In one apartment building after another, mattresses were hanging out of windows; vegetable carts made their way up and down side streets. The rich, charry aroma of potatoes baking in their tin streetcorner ovens wafted over the neighborhood; peddlers walked right up the middle of the street, crying, "I cash clothes." It's a new season; my mother will be twenty in a few weeks.

My mother took one trolley and transferred to another at Burnside Avenue. Jacob, whom everyone called Docky, had an office down the street from his home. Unlike others' businesses during the Depression, his seemed to pick up one year after another. His office was always crowded with important referrals. My mother might have welcomed the anonymity this bustling space provided.

He ushered her into an office decorated with his degrees from Europe, Canada, and the United States. The chairs were leather; the glass-topped desk was mahogany. The place was softly lamplit and smelled faintly of cigar smoke. There were several pictures on the desk; one of them was of her.

It took him no time to diagnose her. He put a stethoscope to her abdomen and heard a heartbeat. When he moved the instrument from his ears to his neck, he smiled.

"Boom-boom-boom, very healthy little socialist child," he said.

My mother wanted to ask him how it was possible to have periods at the same time you were pregnant. But her mind was locked. She saw faces—his; his wife, Lee's; those of her mother, father, sisters—especially the face of her father.

"You can't tell anyone," my mother said.

"What's to tell? I'm your doctor, you're my patient."

"Aunt Lee, my parents, Harriet, anyone!" There might even have been the edge of blackmail in her voice.

"You will have to have the child, you know that," Docky said.

"Just . . . don't . . . say . . . *anything.*"

3.

Pinochle night. Everyone was there. The game took place in the foyer, on the linen-covered table, under a cloud of smoke that drifted up and formed a hazy ceiling above the men. There was a large carousel of colored chips and two decks of coated Player's cards that were constantly being riffled and dealt. The older women congregated in the living room over marzipan, strudel, and coffee, the younger ones were in the back bedrooms, or in a parlor, around a small grand piano, singing songs like "Ain't She Sweet" and "Someone to Watch Over Me."

Every time my mother saw her father she wanted to cry. She avoided eye contact with her parents and with her sister Harriet. Her sister Nancy had large, dark, vacant eyes. Though she smiled at everything, her eyes never did. My mother had no trouble making eye contact with her, or sitting with her while she knitted. It was something of a comfort, watching the ease with which she handled the needles.

There were two relatives she had planned to tell. One was Harriet. The other was Harold, a younger first cousin who had been a sidekick, confidant, and audience for years.

When they were little, they slept in the same bed. When they were a bit older, my mother tried out her stories on him. "Harold," she told him one night, "I just saw the superintendent drag a little girl in off the street. I followed them right into the basement. You know what he did? He threw the little girl into a big furnace and then he shut the door and she screamed and screamed. She was burning up!" My mother was eight, Harold was six. This was on another pinochle night. She yanked him by his shirt, prodded him, poked him, shoved him into the foyer, and then stood lurking in a doorway watching while he inched up to her father at the table and tugged him by the sleeve. The words jumped out of his mouth like frogs.

"Theyputalittlegirlinthefireinthebasementandshe'sall-burningup!"

No one at the table even turned a head.

"Who told you that? Eleanor?"

"Yes! Yes!" he cried.

"I thought so," her father said.

"Play," someone said.

Now the two of them sat at a white enamel kitchen table. My mother had closed the swinging door to the dinette area, which was usually kept open with an angled rubber wedge. She sipped at a glass of scotch and smoked a cigarette down. The story never got to her mouth. The door to the kitchen suddenly burst open and a phalanx of women marched into the room—her mother, Harriet, Aunt Lee.

Harold was asked to leave. The women closed the door behind him and came forward in a wall, positioning themselves at the kitchen table so my mother could not have gotten to her feet if she'd tried.

"Eleanor, Docky told us everything," Lee announced from a vast height, a perennial pince-nez in place, arms folded across an expansive bosom. She was wearing a brooch with an ivory silhouette of the head of someone like Marie-Antoinette that stood out on a dark silk blouse.

"Told . . . ?"

"Eleanor, what in the world is wrong with you?"

"*Told?*"

A cataract of assault and accusation fell on her: "Ruin your life like this!" "Papa, poor papa!" "Deny . . ." "Ruin . . ." "Awful . . ." "Irresponsible . . ." ". . . for the rest of your life." My mother pushed herself to her feet, bumping into the women and knocking them back a clumsy step or two. Though she was still surrounded, it was as if the trap she was in had been momentarily broken, an opening created for just a split second. But the game was up and she knew it. When her mother put a hand on her shoulder and pushed her back down into the chair, she offered no physical resistance.

The women wanted to know who the father was. She would not tell them (she later told Harriet). They wanted to know if the man would marry her. She remained silent. They wanted to know if he even knew. She would not say. They asked if she had plans of any kind, how and where she would actually give birth to a child, by herself, in New York City. She mumbled something about getting a job.

"Job? What are you talking about?" Lee said.

"She's lost her mind," Harriet said.

The room eventually quieted down, and when it did a conspiracy was born.

4.

The goal of the conspiracy was simple: to keep the news at all costs from her father, a sixty-one-year-old druggist who was considered so fragile he might be destroyed if he found out. My mother believed this, too, because in her way she was as fragile as he was. She thought of her father as a dispossessed king and herself as his eternal Cordelia. She thought they were both beautiful wounded beings who needed care and protection. When she closed her eyes, she saw him the way she had as a child, reading aloud at the breakfast table, his eyes shining, his theatrical voice mellifluous and deep. She heard all of *Look Homeward, Angel* from him, all 636 pages: "It was October, but the leaves were shaking. A Star was shaking. A light was waking. Wind was quaking. The star was far. The night the light. The light was bright. A chant, a song, the slow dance of the little things within him. The star over the town, the sod over Ben, night over all . . . O lost! . . . a stone . . . a leaf . . . a door." He had been beaten over the head and left for dead by robbers three different times, he worked sixteen hours a day, he fell asleep at the chess table. But she knew a secret artist in him was still living—in his voice, his mild blue eyes. She was not about to risk harming him.

Lee was the lead conspirator. As the director of a social-service agency in Newark, she had a certain professional authority that matched her strong personality. This was most welcome in a situation where others suspected that a magician's talents would be required to guarantee that the missing

*My great-aunt Lee, the family matriarch, with her husband, Jacob "Docky"
Segal, in the early 1940s*

body of a daughter at home might somehow be overlooked.
She knew the places, the little out-of-the-way homes for
wayward Jewish girls, places in Hoboken and as far away as
Kokomo, Indiana, where a disgraced child could wait out her
time, be delivered by a professional staff, and then be disen-
cumbered of her burden, the bastard child, who would swiftly
and anonymously be placed with the appropriate agencies.
She also had figured out how to keep my grandfather in the
dark.

My mother was to be diagnosed with tuberculosis.
Docky, a TB specialist after all, would make the diagnosis and
the arrangements for her removal to a sanitarium far from the
city, too far for anyone in the family to visit. Meanwhile, a

reservation would be made for my mother in one of these lying-in places; she would wait out her time in safety and then return home after she gave birth. All of this was laid out with a sense of irrefutable logic. How else to arrange for a very compromised young woman to put the past behind her and get on with her life?

My mother wanted no part of homes in Hoboken or Kokomo. She did not want to surrender her child. She wanted her father kept out of it, that was all. So she went along—and did not—at the same time. She had no trouble with the tuberculosis part but told the others she would make her own living arrangements. She would figure out the giving-birth part later on.

There was turmoil over this. Lee said she was being stupid, arrogant, and self-destructive. My grandmother, not as judgmental, was still unable to defend her daughter. She nodded her head almost always when Lee spoke. Harriet could not believe my mother would cavil about any help that came her way. But my mother went ahead with her plan. She had a friend in Manhattan with an apartment who was willing to take her in—for ten dollars a month, less than the cost of one of those homes, she pointed out to her critics.

The women acquiesced because they had no choice, but none of them would have abandoned my mother anyway. The quarreling then boiled down to details, logistics. How would food be taken care of, medical appointments, hospital arrangements? Planning for mail was like blueprinting a bank robbery. The problem was, my grandfather would want to write to his daughter. He would send his letters to the sanitarium she was supposed to be in. Her letters back to him would have to come from that sanitarium. It was days, weeks, before the doctor himself sketched out a good working arrangement whereby letters could be forwarded both ways. The doctor's selflessness, though, provoked the women to a point where the whole conspiracy threatened to unravel. My mother was endangering everyone, not just herself, by continuing to play the heroine. But things did not fall apart.

So one night, at dinner, my grandmother explained to her husband that their daughter had not been well lately, that she had taken her to see Docky, who had examined her and given her a chest X ray, and that the results were not good. My mother watched her father's face actually seem to lose its definition as he took in the news. He was heartbroken. She tried to shut her ears when the questions came. Finally, she left the table, saying she did not feel well, closed herself in her bedroom, and sobbed into her pillows.

After dinner, by prearrangement, Docky and Lee arrived at the house. He had a large manila envelope under his arm, from which he removed an enormous X ray of an obvious pair of lungs. He waved the sheet of film around as he described in technical terms—which he then translated—the etiology of the lesion, the location of the tubercles, how bad it all was. He walked my grandfather over to a chair and sat him down and propped the X ray up with one hand against the light of a table lamp. He leaned over, pointing to one after another of the milky ridges and shadows, explaining everything and how he had already taken it upon himself to make arrangements for Eleanor to go to a sanitarium in Saranac, New York, the best facility in the East, he said, where she would be cured, completely cured within six months.

"*Can* she be cured?" my grandfather asked in a whisper.

The doctor laughed, the patronizing laugh of a professional.

"What a question! Of course she'll be cured, she'll be
cured and she'll come home as good as new. Silly man. Ha
ha ha!"

And so the conspiracy lifted off the ground. The next
day, my mother packed her bags for Saranac and took the
subway to Manhattan, just six miles away.

5.

The next part of the conspiracy really was more about the
young girl's confusions than about anyone's fears for her
father. What to do with an illegitimate child in the closeness
of a Jewish immigrant family in the 1930s? That summer—
1935—was the hottest in recent memory. It is easy to imagine
horsedrawn carts moving with an especially slow and slug-
gish sway up tar-softened streets, of pushcarts being steered
under trees and angled under long flags of shade cut by loom-
ing buildings. There are photographs of the old red-and-
yellow wooden trolleys with their sides stripped and replaced
by gates of summer mesh. Windows up and down the Concourse, everywhere in the city, were lidded with striped
awnings. A day of relief was a walk in the Botanical Garden,
through the lush green near the Lorillard Snuff Mill or in
Central Park, along Harlem Mere seeking the shelter of cool
tunnels or along narrow walks leading to stone bridges, to an
oasis near a sculptured pond.

My mother moved into an apartment on the East Side,

not far from Central Park. I did not know where precisely for almost a decade and a half following her death in early 1984—and then, once again, I came upon this information purely by chance. She lived in an old brownstone building at 131 East 92nd Street. The windows bellied out in the arc of an ornate curved façade decorated with heavy gray masonry. I don't know if she lived on one of the upper floors or in the basement.

The people who saw her that summer, who knew she was pregnant, don't know, either, and have little memory of her state of mind, her outlook. Harriet, one of the triumvirate of helpers who subwayed in from the Bronx to be with her, was vague in describing all details of the confinement. She remembers nothing of her sister's expectations, aspirations, fears. When she talks about this period she conveys a sense of her own distress, not anything of what my mother was going through. Memories of that time crease her brow. Her round, dark eyes seem to grow larger, her small cupid's-bow mouth becomes just a dent in a jaw set with concern. But she can summon up no conversations, no snapshot recollections of days or afternoons spent with her sister. She surmises that my mother stayed close to her apartment because she was fearful that someone on the street might recognize her.

Harold saw her, too. He had for many years a job delivering prescription medicines for a drugstore owned by a distant cousin of the family, and he knew the neighborhood as well as a numbers' runner. During the last years of Prohibition, the packaged medicines he delivered were to Park Avenue swells and consisted mainly of bottles of booze, prepared by the pharmacist who became something of a swell himself on the profits. But Harold was unable to recall the building where

*My mother's sister Harriet in her late
teens or early twenties*

my mother stayed or how she handled the weight of censure surrounding her. For almost anyone living in that era, her behavior was disorienting if not shocking and scandalous.

My mother's oldest friend, Ruth Fletcher, was a Duncan dancer, certainly someone familiar with unconventional behavior. She had been away on tour, had not seen my mother for months when she met her that summer. She said she was startled when she observed my mother's raised, rounded stomach—and heard the story that went with it, about her affair, over now, with a young Broadway actor, Van Heflin. Ruth said she was amazed not because of my mother's condition or because of anything she said, but because she actually seemed to be at peace with herself about it. This was incomprehensible. Ruth said that if she had been in such a position she would have gone insane.

What, then, did my mother think and feel during that strange interregnum? For the longest while, I could not say. It was as though she had disappeared into a Bermuda Triangle, reappearing later, when her ordeal was over. I was left with my imagination—and a lot of old photographs, newspaper clippings, and records of the time, all of which guttered into specifics, into the details of streets and buildings, into the texture of New York then and before, down side streets where buildings today no longer look the way they did then—or no longer exist. Like 131 East 92nd Street. People came and went through a downstairs doorway into a vestibule that had dark mahogany paneling; heavy carpets led up the stairs three flights to apartments, each with a solid oak door. There were brass lighting fixtures on each of the landings, fixtures covered with smoky glass globes. Somewhere in that building, in my mind, is Marion Maurice, the person my mother lived with that summer. No one remembered her. I dimly remember a photograph of her: a large, raw-boned woman with a flat, austere face that might have been painted by Thomas Hart Benton or described in a diary kept by a family heading west through the territories. In this photograph— missing from the box of old family photos I inherited from my parents—the woman is holding me, standing next to a brick wall that looks like the siding of a factory. I remember her in a long, dark winter coat, a dark hat tilted aslant on her head. She looks strong, opinionated, vigorous—and older than my mother. She is smiling at me, beaming down at me in her arms, while I look plumply solemn and thoughtful.

I remember the picture because I once asked about it when I was a child. I was told then that Marion was just a casual friend. My mother said she had known her only briefly and forgotten her last name. When my father* prodded her once, my mother shrugged and said she had heard a rumor, years later, that her friend might have been murdered in a small town somewhere in Pennsylvania. I pestered both my parents about this, because the idea that they might have known someone who had actually been murdered was very exciting. Where was she murdered, how did it happen, did they ever catch the killer? I remember my father sitting there once, concentrated but suddenly silent. My mother jumped in, telling me that she recalled hearing something about Marion's getting involved with a lieutenant on leave from the navy. She lit a cigarette, then extinguished the match with a whip or two of the wrist. Her eyes scanned an imaginary horizon far and near, searching for something more to say that never came.

I remembered this woman's name over the years only because of this vague and grisly half-tale untold by my parents. But the photograph was significant in another way. I believe it was the only one ever taken of me during the time I was in the Home for Hebrew Infants, HHI, an orphanage that went out of business in 1943 but where I lived for the first fourteen months of my life, until my mother claimed me and brought me back to her parents' home, intending to eventually raise me on her own.

---

*I will generally refer to my stepfather as my father, because that is how I knew him; this will change later in the narrative, for the sake of clarity and logic, to distinguish him from Van Heflin.

6.

In July 1935, Harriet phoned the Home for Hebrew Infants, asking if someone there could recommend a good boarding home for an infant soon to be born, pending plans for its later adoption. The person who took the call, according to the record, understood that the woman was not talking about herself and suggested the mother come in and have a talk with people at the home. Instead, Harriet turned up, well dressed, polite, and noticeably edgy.

She said that the child in question would need to be cared for until its adoption. The adoption itself would be arranged by a woman who was in social work in Newark. The interviewer asked Harriet who the mother was. She looked down and fell silent for a long while. "My sister," she said, finally. No one knew about this, she added. Her sister was supposed to be away in Saranac but was living in the city under an assumed name—Eleanor Stone.

My mother gave birth to me using this assumed name at St. Elizabeth's Hospital—in Washington Heights, in northern Manhattan. Some time after that, I was placed in a foster home in White Plains, New York, about twenty-five miles north of the city, but remained there only for a period of weeks, because the cost of maintaining a child in foster care was too high—and I didn't seem to be doing well. I was then placed in the HHI. Though at the outset my mother's family, particularly Lee and Harriet, were clearly determined to have me adopted, it soon became apparent that my mother was not willing to go along. What at first was confusion in her mind soon became a determination to hold on to her child, regardless of what anyone said or did.

I never learned that part of the story while my mother was alive.

7.

By the end, there was one more major conspirator, an aunt, Rose—another sister of Lee's and my grandmother's—who took in foster children to make money and was brought in to help convince my grandfather to do the same. The idea of taking in a foster child was unappealing. Though this was a common practice in working-class Jewish neighborhoods of that era—it was possible to make an extra sixty dollars a month—he wondered how it would be possible to care for someone else's child and then, one day, after feelings were developed, maybe have someone come in and take the child back. Suppose there was something wrong with the child, or it turned out there was a financial burden rather than a gain to be made, what then? So Rose was brought in to go to work on him.

Because she had foster children—three of them—she could point to real successes in her own life. She could talk about how easily she had been able to handle her foster children and how much money she had actually made. She knew the system well enough to sound like an expert, and could refer to all the other families in the neighborhood who had taken in such children and how they had done with them.

She also happened to be a great storyteller and mimic. She would imitate anyone, anytime, improvising body postures and vocal idiosyncrasies at the drop of a hat. She would go to the park, look for a character—the most outrageous she could find—befriend him, talk to him, console him, all for the sake of a story, so she could come home and regale her family with a yarn and a captivating routine. This side of her was what made the others initially reluctant to bring her into the conspiracy. They feared she would let something slip in one of those imaginative, improvisational tirades. But once she was brought in out of need, she did her job. She never proselytized, just told stories. And she brought her well-adjusted foster children with her—one of whom was blond and blue-eyed, something like the child waiting in the wings at the Home for Hebrew Infants.

So my grandfather went along. One day, I—the unidentified foster child—was brought home. I was blond, very blond, and had eyes that looked like blueberries, set in a very solemn face. My grandfather was supposed to have laughed the first time he saw me.

"What's his name?" he asked.

"David," he was told.

My mother had been home for over a year now, recovered from her tuberculosis. But she continued to look pale and puffy, and her spirits constantly seemed to be dragging. However, she was the first in the family to exhibit affection for "the child." She very quickly took to "him" and became my principal caretaker; this fact was observed with pleasure by others, especially her father, who was encouraged by anything that seemed to rouse his daughter from her unsettling lethargy. Some time later, after everyone was used to having a foster child in the house, and long after friends and neighbors had become accustomed to seeing me around, my grandfather was told the truth.

His wife told him one night after dinner, carefully explaining to him why he had been kept out of the loop for so long. He listened in astonishment as the details of the hoodwinking were presented to him, slowly and methodically, like the opening of a nest of Chinese boxes, one opening to the next, opening to the next, down to the little white shoes and tiny sailor blouse on the back of his own grandson.

I can imagine my grandfather at the table at that moment. I can picture the long silence that followed the story, and how he might have lowered his head slightly, gazed forward, chin inclined downward a bit into his chest. When he got angry, his look became dreamy rather than roiled. He had a strange, open face with mild blue eyes and a skeptical brow. This dreamy look of his, however, never failed to frighten his family.

"For God's sakes, Mutya, don't just sit there!" his wife said into the silence at the table.

"Let me understand," he volunteered finally, his low voice a sleepy buzz. "You lied to me, is that right?"

My mother said later that she was frightened not by his words at that moment but by his manner, the tone of his voice, the odd and little arrhythmic ways his body suddenly seemed to move, like a cat in those last steps just before it becomes sick. Afraid he might be having a stroke or a heart attack, she put her hand on his arm. He had no reaction.

"Docky lied to me, Lee lied to me, is that right? The medical reports, the X rays, all lies, is that right?"

"We did this for you, Papa! No one wanted you to be hurt," my mother said.

"For me?" he said. He got up from the table. "You thought it would be better for me to think you had tuberculosis rather than that you were pregnant?"

My mother told me that her father did not blame her but his wife for the betrayal, and that he did not forgive her for the rest of his life.

TWO

1.

In 1935, there were 87,250 births out of wedlock in the United States. These represented a little under 4 percent of the total number of births in the country. In 1997 (the most recent year numbers were reported) 1,257,444 children—32.4 percent—were born to single mothers. Even with a recent decline in such births in this country, the rates here and in other industrialized nations remain eye-catchingly high. Bar graphs can of course be variously interpreted, but what cannot be is the plain fact that single parenting today is commonplace.

It was especially not common for Jewish girls in immigrant families during the 1930s to become pregnant outside marriage. For the devout, the prohibition was absolute and Biblical. For secular Jews, even those who saw themselves as "freethinkers" in a free country, the restraints were just as certain. The traditional family (including common-law husbands and wives, who scorned the bourgeois requirements of legal marriage) formed the brick and mortar of immigrant life, of enduring hard times in a hard and strange land.

For a Jewish woman in the first three decades of the twentieth century in this country, expectations were as narrow as they were inescapable and practical. Hutchins Hapgood, a turn-of-the-century chronicler of Lower East Side life, divided Jewish women into types old and new. The old, or Orthodox, had "no language but Yiddish, no learning but the Talmudic law, no practical authority but that of her husband and rabbi." Whether they were thick-waisted and drab or more attuned to rakish American hats and a willingness to speak English badly, devotion to family and to raising children within the family was absolute. Survival depended on it. The same was true for the "new" type of woman. According to Hapgood, these women "afflicted by modern ideas" were often ignorant except for their readings in socialism; they were rebellious in the manner of advanced Russian thinking; they broke with their forebears in matters of taste, dress, speech, and willingness to assimilate. "Many of these women," he asserted, "lead lives thoroughly devoted to 'the cause' . . . [but] afterwards become good wives and fruitful mothers." On either side of the divide, however, there was no room for a woman to go off and have a child out of wedlock.

Why did my mother do it? What was her thinking—then and afterward? Was she simply panicked after being victimized by a bounder's charms? Or was she a more active and willing participant, maybe the one who did the seducing, both of the lover and then of the man who eventually married her? And if she was the active one, how did she see herself, what were her assumptions and powers? Did she think so much of herself that she believed she could do anything and still have what she wanted in life, or so little of herself that she believed a man's passion for her defined who she was? Why did she so blatantly scorn convention by having a child out of wedlock, hold on to him, and then so completely embrace convention by becoming a good wife and a fruitful mother?

My mother came from a particular kind of family at a particular moment in time. Nothing about her is understandable without this sense of context. When the great exodus of Jews from Europe to the United States began in the last quarter of the nineteenth century, the culture they brought with them was well established. Whether the families were headed by rabbis, scholars, merchants, or political people who barely acknowledged their Jewishness, they shared similar values, including that the father was the head of the household. The weakest and neediest fathers were still deferred to and given the respect of authority.

My mother's maternal family was comparatively well off in the old country. Her grandfather managed the estate of a wealthy landowner in southern Russia. But soon after he settled his family here, on a quiet, shady street in New Haven, he lost everything. A learned man, a splendid singer who was a sometime cantor in the synagogue, he did not speak English, his experience managing an estate meant nothing, and he had little sense of America and its customs. He wound up trying to make seltzer out of tap water in his basement; later, when the family was forced to move to New York, and the daughters got jobs to keep the family going, he was left with a pushcart in a non-Jewish area where he was a frequent target of taunts and fists.

My mother's father came from a different kind of family. His father was a ne'er-do-well—a professional storyteller and a drunk, who drifted from town to town in the old country, selling yarns and collecting wives. It was said that he had married six or seven times, leaving each wife as he moved on with his bag of tales. He may or may not have died of drunkenness or at the hands of a mob, but his son, my grandfather, was raised by one of the wives, who brought him here some time in the 1880s or '90s. She labored to get him through school, instilling in him a love of learning and a sense of paternal responsibility.

At that point, the organization of home life among Jewish immigrants had become as particular as any discrete grouping on earth. The ideas of mutual support, collective effort, the nurturing of the young, especially in the values of family and learning, always a part of Jewish life, were reformulated under the harshness of conditions in the New World. Take the matter of living accommodations, the reality of everyday life on the Lower East Side. Families were suddenly thrust cheek by jowl in close, cramped quarters. "Privacy in the home was practically unknown," wrote Samuel Chotzinoff in *A Lost Paradise*, a memoir of immigrant Jewish life in New York. "The average apartment consisted of three rooms: a kitchen, a parlor, and a doorless and windowless bedroom. The parlor became a sleeping room at night. So did the kitchen when families were unusually large." The kitchen, according to Chotzinoff and, later, to Irving Howe, became the center of life in the home, the metaphoric as well as the actual seat of a shifting center of spiritual and practical power in the family.

In his book *World of Our Fathers*, Howe painstakingly traces the ways in which the patterns of family life, under the burdens and pressures of poverty and underemployment, came to center on the mother and not the father. The father, the traditional head of the household, found it increasingly difficult to make a living, to provide for his family, to maintain his own self-respect. "In the turmoil of the American city, traditional family patterns could not long survive," Howe wrote. "The dispossession and shame of many immigrant fathers has been a major subject for fiction about immigrant Jews both in English and Yiddish." In my mother's home, this great social movement became part of the routine of everyday life.

My mother grew up knowing all about her family's history, the great damage done to the immigrant men, the saving and nurturing efforts and talents of strong women. From childhood, she perceived that her family had been marked in a special way. Her oldest sister, Nancy—fifteen when my mother was born—was retarded, epileptic, plagued by a host of other serious chronic ailments, in need of constant attention. Nancy's illnesses fell across the mantle of the home like a Biblical curse. The parents were bowed by it, my mother grew up shaped by it, moved as much by her parents' constant sorrow as by Nancy's special affliction. Her father's sensitivities—and helplessness—were as visible as daily bread on the table. At times, he seemed almost guilty about the suffering he was helpless to change. Her mother was the one who held things together. It was she who attended to Nancy, who made sure her many needs were taken care of, the right doctors found, the right schools and special classes arranged for. It was a familiar feature of their family life to see the mother pack a bag and leave for a day or two, boarding a bus to another state in search of cures and remedies she read about in magazines.

Harriet had another kind of affliction. She was a musical prodigy. From the day she took her first piano lesson, her hands seemed to have the control of hummingbirds. My grandparents lavished all they could on this girl, who was also a top student and always a willing helper around the house. But her parents' expectation that she would one day concertize was never shared by Harriet, who, try as she did to please her parents, could never get over an innate shyness that made performing in public an excruciating burden. Harriet's teacher, secured for her by her mother, was the noted Ilona Berdachevsky, but even he could not lead the girl past this firewall in her own nature. When he wanted to hear music from her soul, he would remove himself from the room where she was playing, secreting himself in another part of the house. "Play!" he would command, and then sit back and listen to brilliant and melancholy cascades of Chopin, to the amber warmth of Brahms, to the madness of Schumann—all seeming to come effortlessly from a young girl whose passion for playing began and ended with herself.

From the start, my mother worshipped, envied, and resented Harriet. She was her greatest champion. On those few occasions when Harriet did perform, when there was an evening at Washington Irving High School or at Carnegie Recital Hall, my mother could not wait to get to the auditorium; she would dress for the occasion, wear a corsage, hand out programs, greet different relatives and friends with a flood of stories and anecdotes about her sister's playing, many of which, according to Harriet herself, were improvised on the spot.

My mother also came to respect enormously Harriet's distaste for performing, perceiving in it a kind of depth and strength which she associated with the strong women of her clan. Some evenings, my mother would return from wherever she happened to be to find the house empty except for Harriet, sitting alone in the darkness, playing the piano. When this happened, my mother never let on that she was there. She would secrete herself in a doorway and just listen. With all the lights off, Harriet seemed to pour her soul out in the darkness. It was as if Harriet were another person entirely, someone passionate and vulnerable, stormy and unpredictable—all the things she was not in her waking life, when she seemed to be so busy pleasing others—or bossing people around. There was a mystery, a contradiction, in this, which secretly pleased my mother.

The family's fortunes declined over the years. They had to leave a pleasant home on Hughes Avenue for a smaller home, and then for an apartment on the Concourse. The demands on my grandmother had become greater because her presence in the store was increasingly necessary. She had to straighten out a landslide of errors in the books, keeping track of shipments received but not paid for, noting which items were selling, which were not, making sure empty spaces on the shelves were filled, deliveries made on pre-arranged dates. Much of the time, she was not at home.

The day-to-day running of the house, especially the care of Nancy and my mother, fell upon Harriet, who never failed to let my mother know what kind of burden that placed on her. And Harriet was the one who had to interpose herself between my mother and whatever troubles in the outside world she seemed to find herself in, especially in school.

From the start, my mother was a restless, bored, rebellious student. She was a cutup in class, and something of a pied piper, because other children seemed drawn to her, magnetized by her good looks and good nature and by what seemed to be a boundless sense of daring. Even in grade school, boys chased after her. When a boring lesson or a particularly important test was scheduled, my mother would often skip it, turning up in the yard before the day began, chirping confidently about this or that play downtown. There were always two or three friends willing to go along with her.

Increasingly, Harriet was the one who found herself resolving my mother's school problems—something my mother resented yet came to depend on, for Harriet always seemed to get things straightened out. The resentment would come when Harriet questioned her about where she had been, what she had been doing, lecturing her about needing to do well in school.

My mother's school career came to an end in the ninth or tenth grade (it is not clear exactly when—school records for Evander Childs High School for those years, 1929–30, are no longer available; friends and relatives seem unsure as well). I always knew that, but I never knew why. Her explanation for it was a shrug and a joke, family lore—she just didn't like school, she played hooky. But in fact the precipitating incident was this: My mother had a friend in school—Chappie, last name unknown—who was, according to Harriet, a lesbian. My mother apparently became her advocate, shielding her from injustices, real or perceived. One such injustice was a required presence, in uniform, in gym class. Women had to change their clothes in a close, crowded locker room. Chappie, so the story went, did not want to disrobe in front of others, ashamed of having to expose a flat chest—yet was forced to. The girl pleaded with school authorities to let her drop the class but was told the only grounds for an excuse were medical—she would need a doctor's letter to prove she was physically unable to take gym.

That's where my mother came in. She pilfered stationery from Docky. I am uncertain about what she then concocted. It could have been anything from a single crude sentence to a masterwork—replete with allusions to specialists, X rays, and institutions. In any case, she signed her uncle's name to this and gave it to her friend, who in turn submitted it to the appropriate authorities.

No one was fooled—and the trail led to my mother. She at first denied, then admitted to, having written the letter. The matter was serious. Forgery was a crime, said Harriet, who had to go to school to answer for my mother. (My grandmother did not go: she was either too self-conscious about her English or had been kept in the dark.) Harriet explained, many years after my mother's death, that she was present in the principal's office when the decision was made to expel my mother from school.

I have my doubts. For one thing, children were *required* by law to attend school. You were not just "expelled" from a public school as from a private one. For another, no one seems to know what my grandparents thought about having had their youngest daughter cut from the system. In fact, in the years that followed, when my mother was at large on the streets, my grandparents would have had to be unaware of it; Harriet could not explain how my mother was able to come and go without her parents' asking any questions. As far as I can tell, my mother never sat down with her parents and told them there was no graduation on the horizon and that, in fact, she hadn't seen the inside of a school for years.

My guess is that there was not really an expulsion but, rather, a mutual agreement that my mother needed more supervision, more individual attention, than she found in a large public school like Evander. It would have been easy for her—and Harriet—to agree, and then to inform the school that my mother was already in the process of applying to a private school downtown. At one point, my mother actually did so.

Right around that time, my mother's best friend, Ruth, the Duncan dancer, had recently begun attending Walden on a scholarship. Walden, one of the nation's first progressive schools, catered to children with special abilities and interests in the arts. When Ruth told my mother about the school, about all the exciting programs and teachers and how the school was so different from Evander, my mother, without consulting anyone in her family, decided to apply there—in person.

But Walden turned her down. And so she simply stopped going to school—and officials at Evander never knew. Neither did my grandparents, who assumed the metronome of days was as always. But my mother must have been troubled and ill-at-ease in her comings and goings. There was even a time when she was thinking about moving out. One summer, a friend of hers, Max Rosenberg, helped her look for a room in Greenwich Village. They went block to block in the West Village and south of Houston Street. My mother almost took a room in an "artists' boarding house" run by a man named Sundsky, but the rooms were tiny, rodent-infested, and too expensive. It was during the Depression and she could not find a job.

She joined the Young People's Socialist League. I always knew about that. But whenever my mother talked about the YPSL, she did so cursorily, and almost with a sense of apology. When I was growing up, the God in our home was FDR, who incorporated everything the YPSL stood for, she said. I remember the day FDR died. I heard about it in the street. I was nine. I ran home to tell my mother. She slapped me across the face and told me not to make jokes like that. But she turned on the radio, and when she heard the news she began crying—like so many others in the country.

She was an ardent socialist once, believing that human nature was good but capitalism corrupted it. The prescription was simple: get rid of capitalism. When she was just eleven, she kept vigil in Union Square Park for Sacco and Vanzetti. When she was fourteen, she joined Circle 8, Bronx, the largest dues-paying YPSL chapter in the city. Circle Eighters went everywhere, did everything together. They went to rallies and demonstrations, they held dances and went on picnics, taking the ferry at Dyckman Street across to the Palisades and hiking along the cliffs singing songs, dressed in their blue shirts and red ties. They had their own orchestra, a group they named the Cacophonic Symphonic Orchestra, which played all over the city. There was a section for kazoos in the ensemble, and another for those who stretched rubber bands from their teeth. The conductor dressed in long tails, which flew up in climactic moments to reveal flashing lights attached to the seat of his pants.

"Eleanor never knew that much about Marx or Lenin, but she was smart, sexy, and lively," said Rosenberg, one of her old YPSL comrades. Another, Florence Rossi, said that whoever my mother would "shine" on would be hers for as long as she wanted. "Boys didn't pick her, she picked them."

Once a year, my mother would hitchhike to YPSL conventions in other states. There were planks and platforms passed, resolutions to support the imprisoned labor organizer Tom Mooney, or the nine black youths, known as the Scottsboro Boys, waiting on death row, accused of having raped a white woman. Coming back from one of these conventions in Pennsylvania, my mother and her friend Rosenberg caught a highway ride with a big rig. The driver at one point pulled off the road, told Rosenberg to get out of the truck, and then began mauling my mother; with a well-placed elbow or knee, she managed to escape. The two friends waited in the dark, in the underbrush, until first light, when they walked out to the highway and again stuck out their thumbs.

My mother got her sidekick, Harold, to join the YPSL. She took him on his first "action," in the garment district. He was fifteen, she was seventeen. The Socialist Party was then in the throes of organizing on behalf of the ILGWU (International Ladies' Garment Workers Union). The two of them went up a service elevator and got off on a floor that contained a long, open shop where rows of women were bent over their machines. These workers apparently had been reluctant, or too fearful, to show support for the union. There was a switch box full of fuses and wires. My mother opened the box, yanked the wires, and smashed the fuses with a brick, plunging the room into darkness.

She grabbed Harold's hand and together they began running through the room. "Strike! Strike! Strike! Everybody out!" she shouted. When the two youngsters made it down a stairwell to the street, the workers were filing out of the building. The YPSL pickets cheered each of the women workers as they emerged from the building.

There were regular Circle 8 parties at my mother's home. The women always gave ground to the men, who were the theoreticians. But in my mother's group, this deference was performed with a certain flourish of spirited irony. The women had a favorite song, said Florence Rossi, Joe Hill's "The Rebel Girl," which they sang loudly and with great gusto:

> *There are blue-blooded queens and princesses*
> *Who have charms made of diamonds and pearl*
> *But the only thoroughbred lady is the rebel girl*
> *That's the Rebel Girl, the Rebel Girl.*
> *To the working class she's a precious pearl.*
> *She brings courage, pride and joy*
> *To the fighting rebel boy.*

But my mother's socialism was only part of this other life of hers. At a very early age, perhaps by the time she was ten or eleven, she became interested in the theater and was starstruck by the famous actress Eva Le Gallienne. Growing up, I heard my mother mention Le Gallienne's name occasionally. Sometimes when she played hooky from school, my mother said, she would go downtown and sneak into the old Civic Repertory building on 14th Street to watch Le Gallienne rehearse. She made this sound like a prank. She never explained why she liked Le Gallienne so much.

Occasionally, she took her cousin Harold on these forays to the Civic Rep. He recalled that the two of them would sneak into the building in the early afternoon, going up a fire escape that led to a door to the balcony of the theater. They slouched down in seats in the first row behind the lip of the balcony, watching the actors down below on the stage. Le Gallienne was always dressed in loose, flowing slacks and would stop in the middle of a scene to talk with her fellow actors. Or sometimes she would do part of a scene over and over again. To my mother it was like hearing a beloved piece of music repeated again and again.

Le Gallienne was a very special personality in the theater. She was an iconoclast, a radical, and a bohemian. Apart from her superb acting ability, she was a builder and a scorner of convention, both as an artist and in her personal life, where her lesbianism was common knowledge. Completely turning her back on Broadway, she founded the Civic Rep, the nation's first great repertory company and one that led, ultimately, to the Group Theater, which led to the Actors Studio and to the mainstream itself, transforming the texture and style of contemporary theater. Each season from 1926 to 1935, Le Gallienne presented a roster of great plays at a cost anyone could afford. The most expensive seat in a house that held eleven hundred people was $1.60, the least expensive fifty cents. Le Gallienne starred in most of her productions— her performances in *Three Sisters, Hedda Gabler,* and *Romeo and Juliet* are still talked about—but she was also a producer and a director. She was an inspiration to young women in and out of the theater at a time when women realistically saw their future in terms of marriage and family. Le Gallienne's followers, mostly young women—like my mother—were devoted almost to the point of being cultish. They knew the hours when Le Gallienne rehearsed, when she walked to her home on West 11th Street at the end of the afternoon, before that evening's performance. They would walk up and down in front of her house waiting for her to come in or go out, then hand her bouquets of flowers and talk with her as she walked up the street. They were not autograph seekers but devotees, believers not so much in a cause as in a shared dream of themselves as free women, artists, and bohemians.

My mother wanted to be an actress. She told me this once but then shrugged it off, saying she never had the courage to walk into an agent's office. This may or may not have been true; in later life, it served her disguise well enough. That part of her past, even more than her socialism, was almost completely hidden.

Her friend Max referred to the year in which she met Van Heflin and became pregnant as her "*saison*," a period of madness he could explain only as a kind of hormonal excess. He did not know about her love of theater—or did not take it seriously. Her friend Ruth remembers seeing my mother, in her early teens, in a play at the Henry Street Settlement, one of the first off-off-Broadway houses in the city, but she did not remember the play or very much about my mother's acting.

However, in that year of her *saison*, my mother was spending much of her time with new friends she had made in the Group Theater. Her friend Florence, like all her YPSL friends, did not see her then, but heard that my mother had had an affair with an actor—she thought from the Yiddish Theater but wasn't sure—and that my mother frequented places like Stewart's Cafeteria in the Village, a favorite hangout of the Group. In his book *The Fervent Years,* Harold Clurman described the scene at Stewart's:

> At midnight it had the festive air of Madison
> Square Garden on the occasion of a big fight.
> Here the poor and jolly have-beens, ne'er do
> wells, names-to-be, the intellectual, the
> bohemian, the lazy, the neurotic, confused
> and unfortunate, the radicals, mystics, thugs,
> drabs, and sweet young people without a
> base, collected noisily to make a very stirring
> music of their discord and hope.

My mother was somewhere in that very stirring music when she met Heflin, a young actor hanging around with the Group, starting to make his way on Broadway. Strange. In Clurman's book there is a portrait of a young girl, a radical, a waif—unnamed—who meets, marries, and then is divorced by a young actor from Oklahoma—also unnamed—who almost certainly was Heflin. Even more certainly, Heflin was married when my mother met him. He had married an older woman, a screen actress named Esther Ralston, in the summer of 1934. They were divorced in 1936. (He was also briefly married, prior to that, to a young actress named Eleanor Sher, though the dates and circumstances of that marriage remain unclear.) This is how Clurman described the coming together of the unnamed young waif and the handsome young actor:

> This girl, without sufficient funds to fix her
> teeth, too pretty and pushing to remain in her
> proletarian home somewhere in the hinter-
> land, too unprotected to receive proper guid-

ance for her incipient talent, too ignorant to
amount to much without such guidance, too
alive and clean-souled to make any convenient adjustment, and finally too unconcen-
trated because of all this to cut through to a
sane consummation of herself, was living
somehow, nohow, like a fresh plant in the
middle of chaos. She met a handsome boy in
flight from an important Oklahoma family.
What must have seemed to him first an
adventuresome life and background attracted
him to her; and he must have seemed to her a
Western Galahad, strong, educated, and
thoroughly at home in the big American
scene. They were married. In the middle of
the thirties she was "radicalized" along with
others of her age and experience, hung on the
fringes of the Group, acted in the Federal
Theater, where . . . her play was given a trial
performance—and drifted. Her husband
began to get parts on Broadway, disapproved
of her friends (his uncle was a notorious reac-
tionary in Congress), grew successful and
divorced her.

The young woman so carefully described here, perhaps
with some encoding to protect Heflin's reputation, does not
really resemble Esther Ralston. But she does, in some uncanny
way, make me think of my mother and what she might have
gone through—before I knew her.

2.

This is how my mother finally got married. She met a man named Benjamin Siff when she was twelve and he was nineteen. The occasion of their meeting was a mild day at a seaside community in the Rockaways where many immigrant Jewish families took bungalows for a week or two during the summer months. My mother's family had a cottage next to the Siffs'. Both families came from Russia, more or less from the same area south of Kiev. The paterfamilias of the Siff family was a short, balding, irate widower known up and down the boardwalk as a disgruntled ex-Menshevik and ex-friend of Trotsky who had become a successful physician. The paterfamilias of the Segal clan was pleased to be vacationing next to someone so illustrious and invited the man one day to share a glass of tea on the front porch. The glass of tea led to a spirited discussion of socialist politics, and then to a game of chess, and then to a dinner invitation. At dinner, Dr. Siff's only child, Benjamin, met the three sisters of the Segal clan for the first time. With his quick, dark eyes, he scanned them, dismissing the vacant-eyed eldest one, lingering for a moment on the middle sister, who was then sixteen, finally fastening on the twelve-year-old, who, according to everyone in the family, became thereafter the object of his unceasing ardor.

Exactly how this worked was unclear. Ben was volatile but shy. He was also extremely sensible, aware that the difference in age between a respectable Columbia prelaw man and a twelve-year-old girl still skinning her knees and braiding a doll's hair was formidable. He wore bow ties and stiff straw hats, even on hot days in the summer. He was fond of singing Gilbert and Sullivan, of reading the love poems of Robert Browning aloud; these were his calling cards with the opposite sex, but he could not begin to use them with his bewitching child inamorata. Instead he became her tutor in math.

He was a math whiz; she prided herself on having trouble multiplying zeros. Through the summer, then right through the school year and beyond, he came to the house bringing little hand-prepared packets of lessons for her. These were booklets filled with descriptions of algebraic formulas and of how different theorems in geometry worked. Illustrations accompanied them, stick figures in sets, faces smiling and frowning, cows leaping over moons, along with several diagrams set out like little puzzles—"How Does Eleanor Find Her Way Out of Daedalus's Labyrinth (hint, hint: x over y equals 100 yards)"—that a child might enjoy solving. My mother, when she tired of trying to work through a problem and of being treated like a child, would deliberately give him bogus answers, some so tangled Daedalus himself might have been needed to unravel them—just for the pleasure of seeing him become tongue-tied. One night when she was fifteen, the math tutor finally got around to Browning. They were sitting on the front steps of her family's bungalow just after dinner. A moon heavy as a gong lay on the horizon. You could hear the deep sound of the ocean in the darkness a few blocks away. He let himself drift.

" 'The gray sea and the long black land,' " he said, almost as if he were talking to himself, " 'And the Yellow half moon large and low; / And the startled little waves that leap / In fiery ringlets from their sleep, / As I gain the cove with pushing prow, / And quench its speed i' the slushy sand.' Browning," he confessed. "Do you know it?"

"No, I don't," she said. He wanted to go on, but she got to her feet and excused herself, thanking him for the day's lesson. Inside, she took her sister Harriet by the sleeve. "My God, I think he *likes* me!" She was white as a sheet.

"So?" Harriet said.

"What do you mean, 'so'? *I don't like him.*"

It didn't matter. He attached himself, if not to her, then to the house, something like a maiden aunt. He turned up regularly, summer and winter, on pinochle nights, on holidays, a chess partner, Harriet's friend, always willing to do an errand, sing a song, join an ice-skating party, ever ready to help out. After a while, the pretext of math lessons dropped away and he was just there. No one thought twice about coming home and finding him in the living room reading a book.

The day he began driving a cab, he asked my mother if she would like to go for a ride with him. He appeared at the house wearing a cloth workingman's cap rakishly tilted over an eyebrow. She said no. Jaunty and in good spirits, he persisted. He asked her to let him give her a lift anywhere, anyplace she wanted to go. Greenwich Village, she finally said. By then she had lots of downtown friends and spent considerable amounts of time at the Rand School, at Union Square, at Stewart's Cafeteria. She had a coat that buttoned up the back, and bangs with little spinning curls like Lillian Gish's. She laughed when he bowed like a chauffeur and held the door open for her to climb into the rear seat of the cab. He drove her up the Concourse, across the Willis Avenue Bridge, all the way down Second Avenue, and then across 14th Street, never reaching over for that twenty-cent flag drop. They talked

Cinderella's coachman and bon vivant—my stepfather, Benjamin Siff—
when he was about twenty

about law school, the garment workers' strike, the death of
the great socialist leader Morris Hillquit, and about Eva Le
Gallienne, whose theater was about to close.

In 1937, two years after the truth had been revealed,
when the melodrama of the sanitarium, the orphanage, and
the foster child had finally run its course, Benjamin Siff, like
everyone else, could see that Eleanor Segal was an unmarried
woman raising a child alone. He saw that there was no
husband-in-the-wings, not even a boyfriend. His heart
ached. She was as beautiful as ever. And, he could plainly see,
someone who was in real need. Without quite figuring out
the complications there might be for him in pursuing her, he
finally decided to ask her to marry him. He framed the pro-
posal for himself for days. First he tried writing it down, in

verse, in the style of W. S. Gilbert, because he thought it would be easier if it were done in a lighthearted fashion, easier for her—and for him if speech failed. But he tore this up, knowing he had to speak directly. He came over to the house one evening after she had put me to bed and asked if she would take a walk around the block with him. They made one full circuit of the neighborhood before he got around to what was on his mind. He stammered, then went on and on about the difficulty of raising a child alone. He talked about the good job he now had downtown—he was writing briefs, would soon be trying cases, preparing appeals, moving up in his law firm. Finally, he popped the question. He said that he knew she didn't love him but that he loved her and would be a good father to her son, and that maybe in time she would come to love him, too.

My mother was touched by this. She thought about what he said, and also about the way he said it. There was something so endearingly clumsy about him. She could almost feel him blushing in the dark. His hands chopping the air for emphasis, his voice rising an unruly octave or two—all of that got to her, but she couldn't marry someone she didn't love. She said no. Still, she was impressed by his willingness to take on a "damaged" and compromised woman with no seeming regard for what it might mean to him. She found herself thereafter far more willing to spend time with him than she had been before.

On some days, she let him accompany her and me over to Morris Park for an hour of fresh air. These outings were a relief from the constant pressure she experienced at home, where she felt she was a burden and an expense to her parents, something her sister Harriet often pointed out. Sitting on a park bench, she would listen to my father talk about almost anything: the law, his new job, the childhood years he had spent in Russia. He would even go on about recent games of bridge and chess he had played—and it all sounded soothing where formerly she had been bored. He tried to cheer her up, to entertain her. One day he told her that, in the very same park in which they were sitting, in that bathhouse across the way, he and a group of his friends had been playing a game of craps once. He painted the scene for her, the circle of avid faces, the dollars piling up, the old bones rattling against the concrete floor. Then he described a midnight robbery. He was in the middle of a roll, he said, and just then, just when he hit double ten and broke the bank, just like that, in walked three masked gunmen who ordered everyone to the floor. The intruders commanded everyone to strip naked, and then they scooped up pants, underwear, shoes, socks, and loot and fled into the night, leaving them there as pink and exposed as baby chicks. So how did the featherless birds make it home through the streets of the Bronx? He got to his feet and pantomimed dodging in and out of doorways with sheets of the *New York World Telegram* around his hips. He took three funny little sidesteps, four or five doubled over, then stood straight as a sentry to indicate hiding in a doorway from a passerby. She had a good, unthinking laugh.

But it was almost a year before she agreed to marry him, and then with the knowledge that she still did not love him. Her father was working Sundays now, and her mother, to save money, had replaced one of the clerks in the store. Harriet, who had gotten married, was still living in the house with her new husband, Morty. Nancy had recently been diagnosed with cancer. So, one summer day, though Benjamin Siff was unaware of what the gods had in store for him, a series of events took place that brought Eleanor Segal into his life forever.

He was on a camping trip with Harriet and Morty. Back in the Bronx, there was a telephone call one evening from a local hospital, which my mother answered. The call said that Morty's father, a long-term patient suffering with what physicians called cardiac asthma, had become agitated and had to be restrained and taken downtown to Bellevue, where he had suddenly died. Because Morty and Harriet were away, she went to Bellevue to claim the body, to make tentative arrangements for a funeral. Then she left me with her parents and took a bus to Lake George and a taxicab from the bus station to the edge of the campsite where she knew the three of them were staying, to tell them the news. She assumed they would all return to New York immediately. Instead, Morty said he had been worn out by his job and that there would be no harm continuing their vacation for another day or two before returning to make final arrangements for the funeral.

There were two tents. Harriet and her husband had one, Benjamin Siff had the other. Harriet fished out a change of clothes, a towel, and a bathing suit and handed it to her sister. Morty began to gather some things for himself.

"This is the girls' tent, the boys have the other," he said.

"Don't be ridiculous," my mother said. She took the clothes her sister had just given her and marched across the way to the other tent.

The marriage took place two weeks later.

THREE

1.

My parents' wedding took place in Lee and Docky's apartment. Their place was spacious and well furnished, with long sofas and plump armchairs with silk coverings. Set on a perfect linen tablecloth were silver candleholders, stacked plates of white bone china, fine monogrammed silver cutlery, and a family of cut crystal glasses: heavy goblets for wine, lighter ones for water, smaller ones for schnapps after the wedding dinner. But there were no invitations, no guests outside my mother's immediate family.

A down-at-the-heels rabbi, a distant cousin of Rose, my storytelling great-aunt, presided. It is not clear if any relatives of my father's attended or were even invited. The decision to restrict the guest list so severely may simply have been a bow to those pages of wedding etiquette that suggested that, in any union where one of the partners may once have been married or was already a parent, discretion and modesty were in order. But it was also possible that other factors were involved—such as the negative opinion friends might have had about what my parents were doing. My mother's friend Ruth begged and pleaded with her, just days before the ceremony, not to go through with it. She cried, she remembered, when my mother told her she was marrying Ben Siff. She was throwing her life away, Ruth said. No, my mother answered, she knew what she was doing, and asked Ruth please to let her be. My mother's friend, almost half a century later, could not get over what seemed like taking an inexplicable turn against herself and her own happiness.

It was also likely that relatives on my father's side, particularly a first cousin who especially worshipped him, were just as strongly opposed to the union.

When the ceremony was finished, the family drank, sat down to a brief dinner, and then, as if by arrangement, my parents accepted mazel tovs and kisses on the cheek, picked up the small cardboard suitcases previously left in the hallway, and took the elevator downstairs to the Concourse, where they took a taxicab to Pennsylvania Station and then boarded a train to Washington, D.C., for a weekend honeymoon.

When I was growing up, anniversaries were never celebrated in my home. There were no pictures of the wedding— or of any anniversaries. Neither my brother,* sister, nor I ever

*Throughout, I will refer to all my half siblings as brothers and sisters.

asked questions about this. My brother, Daniel, believes this
was in accord with a culture of modesty in our house. But it
was also in accord with a culture of secrecy and a willing
blindness.

I can imagine just how difficult it was for my parents to
celebrate an anniversary openly. To have had an uncomplicated tenth-anniversary celebration, say, they would have
had to set up a charade, because in reality they would only
have been celebrating their eighth anniversary. Their actual
wedding date—two years after my birth—was a cornerstone
of the secret.

In their lifetime, my parents never talked about their
honeymoon—other than to say they went to Washington.
When any of us asked them about it, they would shrug it off
with a tilt of the head, a turning up of the palms, a wisecrack
or two. Washington's Washington, they would always say.
What was not mentioned—ever—was that during this trip
my father suddenly became ill, suffering waves of sharp pain
in his lower abdomen. My mother decided to cut the honeymoon short and return to New York. She insisted, despite his
protestations, that he be examined immediately. He was
diagnosed with acute appendicitis and scheduled that day for
surgery. She escorted him to his hospital room, sat with him
before he was wheeled away, and was there when he was
returned.

Why would they have kept all that secret? The best
explanation I can offer, poor as it is, is that the event created a
hospital record, a paper trail that might have led to a discovery at some future date that they were married two years after
I was born.

The first apartment I remember living in with my parents
was on Morris Avenue in the Bronx, just across the way from

a spacious, open park with tennis courts. We lived on the ground floor, and my grandparents and Nancy lived in another ground-floor apartment, just across the courtyard entrance to the building. My parents frequently went over to visit. They had dinner there several times a week, often tucking me into my crib and letting me fall asleep before they went. The earliest memory I have is waking up in my crib at night with no one home, screaming into the slashes of light coming through the venetian blinds of the bedroom window—until my mother came rushing back from the other apartment. I knew nothing about the cross-courtyard intercom system—open windows in both apartments—she later swore she had.

I also did not know that her life then was caught up not so much in her new marriage or in raising her child as in the fact that her sister Nancy had developed incurable cancer. All our lives were altered by this.

At first, I was aware only that my mother often brought me to my grandparents' apartment to visit during the days. I was presented to Nancy, asked to sing songs that my mother had taught me at bedtime, or just to be present for Nancy's sake, to stand there or to sit next to her and let her tousle my hair. Her room, I remember, had a bitter smell, like rubbing alcohol. There was a big table filled with medicine bottles, syringes, an enema bag, stoppered bottles with residues of brown liquid in them. When I sang my songs, I was praised by everyone in the room, so I did not mind too much. But when Nancy wanted to take me outside by herself, to take me for a walk or to go to the playground, I was always glad that my mother trailed close behind, so that if I wanted I could pull away and run to her.

One day, Nancy announced that she wanted to have a

picture taken with me. She wanted a keepsake of the two of us, she said, to place next to her bedside so she could look at it when she was lying there. It would be like having me with her, my mother explained. Nancy had gotten much sicker by then.

So my mother arranged this. She had Morty, owner of a fancy new Kodak camera that opened from a slimline case into a bellows lens with a cable trigger, do the job. My mother dressed me in my best little sailor suit—a blue cotton blouse swimming with white polka dots, insignia designs of anchors, and a little flap of collar that dropped behind my neck like a turned-around bib. The living room in my grand-parents' apartment was pulled apart and rearranged so Nancy and I could be posed in a window alcove that provided dra-matic lighting. When I was placed on her lap, however, I fled—down the hallway, into one bedroom and then another, until I was caught on the edge of a window about to dive out.

"David, they're taking *your* picture, behave yourself!" my mother snapped, jerking me back into the room. She took a comb out of the pocket of her slacks and wrenched knots out of my hair.

"Make your aunt happy, make her happy for me," my mother whispered in my ear, making her last adjustments of blouse, buttons, and hair before turning me over to my father, who hoisted me into the air.

"Then give three cheers, and one cheer more for our little captain of the Pinafore," he sang as he flew me nearly ceiling-high from the back bedroom to the living room and the land-ing strip of Nancy's lap.

Snap! Picture taken.

"Over here, David!" said my mother. She was on the other

My mother's sister Nancy in her twenties

side of the room, her head suddenly coming up like that of a jack-in-the-box from behind an armchair. Picture taken, boy and aunt both laughing.

When my mother was eleven, she had already assumed some of Nancy's caretaking. A friend of my mother's remembered that one afternoon she and my mother took Nancy to the movies. They took the bus up the Concourse, got out on Fordham Road, a couple of blocks from the old Keith's Theater. My mother gaily marched them up the street as though she were a lowly deckhand who had wrangled a day of shore liberty for them.

In those days neighborhood movie-theater shows regularly included live vaudeville. The shows started at one in the afternoon, ended at five. In between double features of

Valentino and Theda Bara and Scott Joplin rags, the house lights came up to half for acts like Willie Howard and the Sunshine Boys.

That day, Nancy had a grand-mal seizure in the middle of one of the vaudeville acts. She was foaming and drooling as she crashed around on the floor, wedged between the seats of one row and the next. The show stopped, everyone onstage and in the house turning to look. My mother and her friend searched for shadows but there were none, so they dived into the aisle and ran for it—out of the theater and up the street, fleeing as far and as fast as their spindly legs could carry them. An hour later, Nancy was brought home on a stretcher in the back of a Fire Department ambulance.

Watching from a hiding place in a doorway nearby, my mother, clinging to her friend's neck, said, "I think she died."

My mother's friend, who wishes to remain unnamed, said that she has carried guilt from that day to the present; she is in her eighties. My mother never spoke about the incident.

Now, as Nancy grew more ill, my mother decided that the courtyard apartments should be abandoned and that all of us should be housed together under one roof. We all moved to a larger apartment on nearby Sheridan Avenue, not too far from Claremont Park. I assume that my mother engineered this because she felt she needed to offer her parents relief so they could get on with their own troubled and busy lives. But I also imagine that some special feeling about how she had once failed her dying older sister was involved as well. My mother stayed at home with Nancy until her parents got back from the store and my father returned from his office.

My mother tried as best she could to shield me from what was going on. I was kept out of Nancy's room. When it was time for dinner and Nancy was brought out of her bedroom to the table, my mother made sure I did not witness this diffi- cult transit. I was invariably taken to my bedroom to pick up my toys, or to the bathroom to wash up, coming to the table only after Nancy was seated.

Quiet was the rule in the house. No running, no shout- ing, no turning up the radio. Whatever dampening effect this had on me, my mother, I could sense, was in her own special world of sorrow. I'd see her in the living room and know she was unhappy about something. Sometimes I'd just stop what- ever I was doing and watch my parents both lean forward on their elbows on either side of a thin round mahogany table, listening to a tall cathedral radio that had glowing tubes inside that smelled like dust cooking when they were lit up. When my parents listened to the radio, I thought they were listening to different programs at the same time. My father would sometimes lean back from the mahogany table, laugh- ing, while my mother kept leaning on her elbows looking as though she weren't even in the room.

One day, I got up and there was bright light in the hall- way. All the bedroom doors, including Nancy's, were wide open, as was the bathroom door at the end of the hallway. Sunlight streamed in from the bedrooms out to the hall, from the bright parlor down the long corridor. I went to my mother's room, where she was dressing herself before a mir- ror. She was in a slip, and her dark hair was wound tightly in a bun in a net on top of her head. She was leaning toward the mirror, carefully daubing lipstick around the puckered circle of her open mouth, working the lipstick in with closed lips, then blotting her mouth with a piece of toilet paper. When she saw me, she closed her lipstick tube, put it down, and lifted me up in her arms. I could smell fresh powder on her body. She carried me over to the bed, where she sat down, standing me in front of her. She gave me a kiss.

"David," she told me, "Nancy died last night." Then she warned me to say nothing to my grandmother.

I had no reaction to this. But my mother must have thought I did. She hugged me so hard I nearly lost my breath. I remember pulling away from her and then, when I was free, skipping down the hall to tell my grandmother what I had just learned.

2.

We lived in the apartment on Sheridan Avenue for only a short while after. It was early 1941. We moved then into a larger place on the Grand Concourse—once again, with my grandparents. Why my parents continued to share rather than take an apartment for themselves was never clear. Perhaps my mother simply wanted to have her mother in the house to help her with the day-to-day routine of cooking, cleaning, and looking after *two* small children—several months before Nancy died, my brother, Daniel, was born.

We moved into the building where Lee and Docky lived, the same one where my parents had been married. It was a large, impressive building with an impressive-sounding name—the Louis Morris—all in white, smooth brick, towering over the Concourse. I had a room to myself in the front of the apartment. There was a large kitchen, a larger foyer, a still larger living room, and a long, dark hallway with two more bedrooms, one for my grandparents and one at the far end of the hall for my parents and brother, who was still in a crib.

My mother had her hands full. She did the shopping for the family, had her children to look after, did what she could in the kitchen, which my grandmother presided over as her own duchy. My grandmother returned home in time to prepare dinner, which all of us had together. After dinner, my mother, helped by her mother, busied herself with the children, mainly with my brother, changing him, bathing him, getting him ready for bed. My father did the dishes, then joined my grandfather in the living room to read the evening papers. My father was a chain-smoker, my grandfather smoked an occasional cigar. One man lost himself in the *New York Post*, the other in either the *Day* or the *Forward*. Occasionally a discussion about politics would develop, either carried over from the dinner table or sparked by something in the papers. Very occasionally, they would play a game of chess. My father, a much better player, was bored playing anyone he could beat easily. I knew that even then—just from the look on his face. My grandfather took forever over the simplest moves, and all the while my father fidgeted, looking off into the distance, taking quick, impatient puffs of his cigarette. I was introduced to *The Lone Ranger* then—a way to keep me occupied. My father looked up the program in the paper one evening, switched on the radio, then sat me down in front of it. It was like leading an ant to a honey jar. The program was on three times a week, and the other days I picked up *The Green Hornet* and then, later, a slew of other "regular" afternoon programs—*Jack Armstrong, the All-American Boy; Tom Mix; Superman;* and then my favorite Sunday drama, *The Shadow*.

My mother must have been overwhelmed in this setting—not just owing to her youth and inexperience. She was surrounded as never before. Lee and Docky were constantly present. Harriet and her husband lived just down the street and we saw them all the time. I never saw my mother with a friend outside the family in those days. Friday nights, as in her childhood home, there was the usual gathering until late for cards, cigars, and drinks.

Her cares as a mother were now divided between the basic but special attention she had to give to an infant, and that required for me. I took to my new brother in ways that must have seemed disturbing. Apart from the usual and predictable signs like rocking his carriage in triple time to get him to sleep, or burping him a little too hard when I was allowed to hold him, there were other, more troubling signs.

One day, when I was watching him in my room, I took my favorite toy, a silver-colored metal airplane with four spinning propeller blades and landing wheels under the wings and tail, and pitched it out the window to a courtyard eight stories below. Knowing that my brother was not yet able to speak, I worked myself into cascades of tears and went to get my mother, dragging her by the hand back to the bedroom. I told her Daniel threw my favorite plane out the window. I pointed out the wreckage to her in the courtyard below. I waited for her to administer justice. My mother, of course, knew that my brother could not have committed the crime I accused him of, but in order to appease me, she pretended—very gently—to scold him. She lightly tapped him on the behind a couple of times and then had the two of us join her in the kitchen, where she could watch *me*.

I had become moody, needy, and quite unpredictable. In

school I became obsessed with having to write right-handed like everyone else. When I tried to get my mother to sit with me while I practiced, she would not do it. She simply pointed out how much easier it was to use my left hand.

I had a friend in my building to whom I regularly gave away my best toys. I could not help doing this; it was the only way I could think of to keep the friend. When my mother found out, she had the good sense not to ask the boy's parents to give the toys back, but she did ask me why I was doing it. I denied giving away the toys.

I used to play war games with friends in the building. Every afternoon, after school, we would go to a large vacant lot next to our building and pretend we were soldiers. We had a general, an eight-year-old, a couple of years older than the rest of us. One day, when he had to go to the store for his mother, the other boys said I could be the general. My battle plan was to ambush the evil old general when he returned from the market. But the ambush, at the last minute, was turned on me. We were crouched down behind a wall, ready to spray pebbles on the target. With a whistle and hand signal from someone else, *I* was showered with fistfuls of pebbles. My former friends, laughing, pleased with themselves, then clambered down an embankment to an area where they camped for an afternoon of games in the dirt. I was left alone, up above, to lick my wounds and learn my lesson. Instead, I picked up the largest rock I could find and flung it down the side of the hill. It struck one of the boys in the head. The others looked up to where I was standing. I ran off.

The boy's mother came down to our apartment that evening and told my parents what had happened. I listened from the hallway as she told them how lucky it was that her son had not been fatally or seriously injured. Afterward, my father summoned me to the living room. My grandparents and my mother were also sitting there. I put on a hangdog appearance, lowering my head and beginning to cry when the first questions were asked. My mother got up from where she was sitting and came over to me, whispered something to my father, and then walked me to my room. When we got there, she sat on the bed and smoothed my hair. She told me I had done something wrong, that she knew I didn't really mean to hurt anyone but that I could have, that I could have hurt someone very badly. Did I understand that? "Yes," I murmured, unable to say what was in my heart: that, when I threw that rock, I hoped it would kill someone. She brushed my tears away, then hugged me.

"Poor David," she said.

I did not really understand the rage that was in me, and I hoped it would just go away if I simply didn't think about it.

It is altogether usual for little boys to get into mischief. Boys can be rambunctious, especially in company, when they need to show off or prove to others how brave, rebellious, or foolhardy they can be. But I also got into trouble when I was by myself, without the need to prove anything to anyone. My parents had a cat. I loved this cat, played with him all the time. One evening, in my room, with the door closed, I tried to stuff him in the back of a toy bus. The bus was about the length of the cat's body and was open at the back. The cat struggled so that I nearly broke his leg as I forced him into the cylindrical steel casing. My mother later asked me if I was thinking about how the cat felt when I did that. The thought had never crossed my mind.

Another time, when I was home from school, playing

outside by myself, I set off a fire alarm. I knew I shouldn't, but I stepped up on the backrest of my tricycle, pulled down the lever, then pedaled away as fast as I could. When I got upstairs, I told my mother I had come in because there was no one outside to play with. A short while later, the doorbell rang. There were men's voices at the door. I went to the back of the apartment, to my parents' bedroom, and listened. Soon I heard the clump of feet in the hallway. I closed the door. My mother opened it—and there were firemen in their black rubber coats, huge boots, and winged helmets. I pretended not to see them. I flew an imaginary plane around the room, making propeller sounds as I tipped my outstretched arms this way and that.

"David, did you set off a fire alarm?"

"Zzzzhhhzzhhh. No. Zhhhhhzhhh."

"David!"

"I said *no!*"

My mother said something to the firemen, who finally turned around and followed her, clumping back up the hall. Then, when she returned, she sat down next to me. She wiped my face.

"Why did you do that, David?" she asked. I buried my face in her blouse.

"You're not supposed to do that, don't you know that?"

I said nothing. She reached her hand under my chin and made me look at her. "I know you didn't mean it, but you can't do things like that." I nodded and, because I could think of no better way out of the mess I was in, looked as sorrowful as I possibly could.

In her book *The Children You Gave Us*, Jacqueline Bernard traces the impact of institutional care on the lives of children in New York Jewish orphanages during the last century and a half. Citing specific articles and studies, she briefly focuses on the Home for Hebrew Infants during the twenties and thirties, the very place, at the very time, where I spent my first year. In one popular article of the day, a writer noted that the typical three-year-old in the Hebrew Home was "unable to talk, except for a few unintelligible words; shuffling and dragging his feet, his jaw dropped in the vacuum of his expression; lacking even the elementary knowledge of the normal eighteen-month-old baby in the poorest home; completely apathetic, or else so desperate in his need for affection and attention that the average adult could not handle his problems."

One of the studies found Hebrew Home children, after only brief incarceration, to be "hyperactive, hostilely aggressive, selfish, uncontrollable, and demanding of special attention. Central to their problems seemed to be an insatiable need for affection with no ability to either accept or return . . . love." And still another study said that by the age of three the children became "hyperkinetic and distractable . . . completely confused about human relationships, and tell of a half a dozen mothers and fathers and say everybody is their brother and sister. . . . They love only themselves and lose themselves in a destructive fantasy life directed both against the world and against themselves."

When I think of my mother then, my imagination leads me back to those reports. Did she see them, did she connect them with my behavior? Yes, I tell myself, on both counts. She saw them—not because she tracked them down herself, which she might have, but because they were more likely put into her hands by her aunt and her sister, social workers for

Jewish care agencies. I can see both these women, before my case was settled, telling my mother to read the reports, urging her to pay attention to them, to think of the consequences— for herself, her family, for the child himself—of holding on to her child rather than surrendering him for adoption.

FOUR

1.

We moved from the Bronx to the Inwood section of Manhattan when I was seven. It was the first time my parents and their children had a place to themselves. The building we lived in was part of a complex of red brick fireproof buildings with silver Art Deco canopies surrounding an inner garden. Our apartment was small. There were two bedrooms—my brother had the larger one, I had the other, and my parents slept on a wide bed in the sunken living room which, during the days, was a combination sofa and wrestling mat. Everyone seemed to tumble onto the bed—to listen to the radio, read, do crossword puzzles, get into tickling fights or long conversations.

It was during the war. On Sunday mornings, I got my brother up early and pulled him by the hand out to the foyer just above the sunken living room. There was a maple drop-leaf table whose legs and frame underneath served as the interior of a B-17, the bomber that saved America. I would wedge my brother into one of the sections below the table, and I would get into another. I was Colin Kelly, he was my bombardier. I don't remember where we flew and who we bombed.

I had a hard time then. In general, I didn't want my brother around—I didn't like the attention he got. I sometimes crept into his room to wake him up and feed him Mallomars that I had spiked with pepper. I stole money from my parents. My father left bills and change out on top of the drop-leaf table; my mother's purse was there as well. I counted out only what I thought I could get away with, so I could come back and do it again.

My mother's time was mainly taken up by my brother—and Harriet. My aunt and uncle moved into the same neighborhood with their first child, a boy, my brother's age, a built-in friend. The two sisters, with their playground-age children, spent almost every day together in the park. I was jealous. And I felt strangely sad when my mother read me books that were supposed to make me feel special even though I was small—like *The Little Engine That Could* or *The Great Gray Bridge and the Little Red Lighthouse*. She read me *Ferdinand the Bull*, the story of the very peaceful bull raised to fight in bullrings who wanted only to lie down in fields and chew on flowers. She didn't see the dangerous and cunning arena warrior in me.

And I didn't see her.

I became aware of my father then, in ways that I had not been before. I had always known that I could get what I wanted from my mother. All I had to do was play the victim. If there were complaints about me in school or from a neighbor, I needed only to explain how I had been wronged and my mother would offer comfort and understanding. If I found it hard to go to sleep and neither of my parents would respond if I called them, I would make myself fall out of bed, hitting the floor like a sack of potatoes. My mother would then come from the other room, pick me up, and, instead of scolding me, make sure I was not bruised or hurt. She would sit with me and put her arms around me, rocking me back and forth for a few moments before sliding me back under the covers, waiting with me until I finally went to sleep.

The first memory I have of my father was when we were both sick with chicken pox, placed in the same bedroom to recover together. It was only months after my parents married. The two of us were waited on hand and foot by my grandmother and mother, as though he were a sultan and I his little prince. I remember the room, the smell of it, the yellow light from the lamps around his bed, and the look of his knees raised under the covers like the humps of a camel. And I remember my mother sitting and whispering to me to be quiet, not to do anything to hurt Daddy's ears.

My father had an almost phobic reaction to noise. Loud sounds would startle him as if he were a rabbit or a racehorse, steady or monotonous ones would drive him crazy. Any noisy game in my room, the high jump or Columbia football, would trigger brief but intense outbursts. At dinner, if ever my brother and I began arguing with my mother or with each other, there would inevitably be a moment when his face

My stepfather at his desk in the late 1940s

would go red, his cheeks would become rigid, and his lips pressed so tightly together you could feel his teeth clamped behind them. "Just *stop* it!" The words would explode through his teeth, coming from some raw, strangled place in his throat. There was silence afterward.

Frightening as it was to me, I never saw this side of him as anything but usual, what any boy's father would be like in the privacy of his own home. When the fits of fury would pass, he was not at all a threatening person but someone I attached myself to easily, trusting, as surely as I did with my mother, that I could take advantage of him. I knew he knew that I stole his money. He never said anything. He would get a grim and settled look on his face when I tried to pry the sports section of the paper loose from him—but he would always surrender it. When it was his turn to put me to bed, I remember how much I looked forward to his telling me a story. He told me about soldiers coming out of the belly of the Trojan Horse and about the Labors of Hercules. One night he told me the story of Joan of Arc. When he got to the part where Joan was burned at the stake, he described the flames licking up around her body from the stack of fagots at her feet. The flames mounted higher and higher, Joan's face began to perspire, the flames rose and rose, yellow and red with black smoke swirling underneath. I could almost feel the skin on Joan's legs begin to sizzle and char. I began to cry. My father stopped. He patted my head. Then he said something about clouds in the sky, a storm gathering, and then, his voice filling with wonder, there was thunder and lightning and it began raining so hard all the fires went out, Joan was saved, and the people came and untied her and took her down and carried her home, and no one was ever burned at the stake again.

But my father's temper was uncontrollable, and it was never clear what set it off. Sometimes there would be a scream from somewhere in the house. I'd open the door to my room just in time to hear a roar from him as he left the apartment, slamming the front door behind him. Ten minutes later, he would be back, looking as quiet and large-eyed as a lost sheep.

Much of the time his anger seemed directed at me, and this too was so unpredictable it went beyond any possibility of preparing a defense. One evening, my mother wanted me to take a bath. I hated baths in those days, and not even the bribe of a toy submarine that could submerge in bathwater and go from one end of the tub to the other powered by a motorized propeller could change my mind. On this one evening, I was standing in the bath as the water was running in, saying something to the effect that the submarine didn't work. My mother called out from wherever she was that I should just take my bath.

"The submarine's broken," I wailed.

With that, my father suddenly burst into the room, his face dark and tight. Before I could say a word, he hit me as hard as he could across the face. I don't know if his hand was open or closed, because the force of the blow was right across the bridge of my nose. That crazy, strangled sound in his throat and the sudden blaze of light in my brain disoriented me. The next thing I knew, my mother was there in the bathroom, telling him to leave, trying to push him out the door. My face felt warm and sticky. I put my hand to it, feeling the wetness. And then, when I looked down, I saw that the ankle-deep running water in the tub was streaming red. I wailed and rapidly jumped up and down as though I were standing in an icy fjord or on a bed of coals.

Another time, my father struck me and called me a Nazi—I don't remember why. He had other names for me: Hottentot, *vantz*, horse's ass. The names spilled out only during eruptions of temper and might be, within minutes, revised with a kiss or a pat on the cheek.

I strangely mistook his rages for a kind of strength. Because they dominated our home, it just seemed logical that he was the strong one in the family—which was not the case. Over time, I tended to focus on who he was, where he came from, what had happened to him, not paying that much attention to my mother. My father's life seemed mysterious and romantic. He was conceived when both his parents, political prisoners, married in Siberia. Peasants in the area, always kind to newlyweds, helped them escape, and when they finally got to New York and my father was born, his mother died in childbirth. He was then raised as a Russian, not an American, by a widower whose only passion was politics. His father's intention, always, was to return to Russia to complete the revolution that was already under way. The famous Dr. Ziev or Siff would be needed in the new order. He had been Trotsky's tutor in Marxism, a friend and ally—before Trotsky once and for all became a committed Bolshevik.

When my father was nine, after he had picked up English on his own and was comfortable in schools here, the 1917 revolution broke out and the widower gathered the boy and set out with him to take a post—minister of education—in the Kerensky government. By the time they got there, social democracy had been replaced by civil war. At one point, the boy and his father lost each other in a railroad station and did not meet up again for days. The boy wandered through a strange little Russian town with wooden sidewalks, taken in by a family whose children played games of kickball with the skulls of slaughtered animals.

When father and son were finally reunited, they became fugitives in their own country, in flight from the armies of both the Reds and the Whites. They moved from town to town, region to region, sleeping in out-of-the-way hostels and boarding houses, fearful that anyone they met might be the agent or spy who would betray them. At night, they lay side by side in bed and communicated to each other by tapping each other's forehead rather than by speaking and risking being overheard through wafer-thin walls. They made their way south to Odessa and the Black Sea, and caught a boat there to Turkey—the last one, so it was said, that left that port until the end of the civil war. The boy would never forget the sights and sounds of fighting on the dock, as the boat moved out from its slip, gunfire coming from somewhere in the maze of streets around the waterfront, men crouched down behind barricades, barrels, buildings, firing back into the city.

We had almost nothing to do with my father's family. It never occurred to me that this might have had to do with me—or, that is, my mother, who blamed my father's father for emotionally damaging his son and, above all, for telling him that he was marrying beneath himself when he chose my mother, an uneducated woman saddled with an illegitimate child. My mother never forgave the Siffs. She had stories about every one of them. Some of the stories may have been true, and some surely were not.

It was my mother who ran our house, just as my grandmother ran hers, just as Lee, Rose, and Harriet ran theirs. My father worshipped my mother; she could do no wrong. My mother, for example, was a terrible cook. She hated the kitchen and the labor of preparing meals. Her idea of dinner was a cow's tongue boiled pink to a point of decomposition and served with barely warmed frozen lima beans and french fries soggy as paper. Or something she called stew: a medley of meat lumps, skinned potatoes and peeled carrots, salted unmercifully and boiled. There was a uniformity of hardness between meat and vegetables, and the thinnest of juice, which had the metallic tang of lukewarm tap water.

But my father would tolerate no criticism of these meals. My brother and I would poke fun; my father, like Sir Walter Raleigh, would throw down his cape for my mother. Anything she cooked was memorable, delicious, unforgettable. To prove it, he would sit there having seconds, thirds, as much as it would take to prove to us what barbarians we had been. The only time he ever criticized anything that came from her kitchen was once when she had run out of coffee and had to use the grinds left over from the last potful. He took a sip of this brew, smiled a winning, crooked smile to let her know in advance that he was just kidding, then asked, very sweetly, "Eleanor, do you like this better than coffee?"

My father depended on my mother. She bought all his clothes, dressed him, matched his ties with his suits. She slowed him down at the kitchen table, cutting his nervous, rapid-fire talk about law and lawyers by coaxing him into playing Twenty Questions with us. He looked to her for vacation suggestions, when to visit and be visited by family, what he should do to keep his children amused and occupied. And though I did not see it then, I know that he leaned on my mother for support at work, where his employers were constantly exploiting him, even abusing him. I suspect he needed her in those years to rouse himself from moods he could not begin to explain to himself. Years later, my brother and I used to tease him about his Russian melancholy.

My mother didn't tease him. She tried to get him to see a psychiatrist. And because he worshipped her and leaned on her so heavily, he went to one—even though he knew it would never work out. He didn't talk about himself. He didn't believe in it. He was a worrier and an exploder, but not a talker. I asked him once, many years later, if he was happy. "Happy? What's happiness? Happiness is freedom from worry," he said. "I've been worried all my life." He lasted two weeks in therapy.

2.

Some time in 1943 or 1944 (my sister, Judy, born in March 1944, was not yet on the scene), my father wrote a letter to my mother's cousin Harold, who had moved to Washington and begun practicing law. It is the only surviving letter from the period in my father's life when my mother tried to push him into analysis. The persona of the letter-writer is Gilbert and Sullivan, the person underneath is a lost cousin of the Brothers K.

"The news I have is of infinite variety," he writes,

> from the sublime to the most sublime. For instance . . . my good wife has sprained her backside so violently that I have been compelled to purchase a steel and whalebone corset for her to enable her to walk upright. About the only consolation I get from the entire affair is that her virtue is safe from the designs of any but the most expert cracksman. Upon first viewing the device I was moved to tears and then to poetry:
>
> > *To think that 'neath this steel and whalebone mesh*
> > *Lies succulent and juicy female flesh,*
> > *Flesh I cannot touch or see*
> > *Unless I first obtain a Segal key.*

He had something to say about my brother and me.

Shall I tell you that David has become a football fan of the most virulent kind; that he speaks, drinks, eats and dreams of nothing else but football. That he plays football every day. That his only ambition in life now is to play fullback for Columbia, no other college will do. That he sings Columbia songs all day long. That by telling the guard at Baker Field that his old man was a former Columbia football player he is admitted into the stadium every day to watch Columbia practice—or shall I skip it?

Or shall I tell you a *chochma* about Daniel? Why not. You are too far away to say no. David was bad and I decided to give him a lecture. I put him on my knee and spoke thusly: David, why are you so bad? Why don't you behave? Why do you grieve your parents so? Why do you make them angry? Why don't you behave?

I continued in this wise for some time. Daniel in the meantime was standing at my side, open mouthed and all ears. I finally concluded, "Look, David, what would you do, if you had a son who behaved the way you do?" David fetched a sigh that seemed to come from his toes and with that affecting sadness which he can turn on so well, replied, "I would send him away." To this I answer that I did not want to do any such thing, that I loved him too much, etc., etc.— and I exacted a worthless promise from him to behave and sent him on his way. I relaxed and Daniel thereupon poked his pudgy fin-

ger into my midriff and said, "Talk to *me*,
daddy." I put him on my knee and went
through the same rigmarole . . . and concluded with the same peroration, "Daniel,
what would *you* do if you had a son who
behaved like you do?" The little pie-faced
abortion looks at me and says, "I would jump
out the window." Blackout.

If this is the kind of stuff you want in a
letter then confirm by return mail. If you
want philosophy just let me know. If you
want what David calls "love stuff," speak to
my wife.

Your most doting cousin by acquisition,
Ben

What I remember from this time is that my mother
couldn't get out of bed. She had what was called a "sacroiliac
back" and would spend hours in the living room lying down,
reading, sipping a drink, or just seeming to stare off into
space. She had that special corset my father wrote about. It
looked like body armor and could stand on the floor by
itself.

I assume my mother went to doctors about her back—
but I don't know this for sure. What I know now is that she
turned to counseling for herself. Beginning in this period, she
began seeing a Viennese-trained psychiatrist named Esther
Menaker. She saw Menaker regularly for a period of years,
then, much later, for another extended period.

When I visited Menaker's office years after my mother's
death, I had the uneasy feeling that I had been there before—
as a child. I waited in a small alcove dimly lit by a single over-

head lamp covered with a jade-green shade. A folding table with a vase of flowers and a mirror behind it was on one side of the room, a small oil painting, eerily familiar—a landscape of house and trees—was on the other. When I met Menaker, her face was familiar. Even though she was ninety-three, she looked many years younger. There wasn't a glint of gray in her sleekly coiffed mahogany-colored hair. She dressed immaculately, silk blouse, tailored skirt. Her skin had the texture of waxed fruit and was speckled with liver spots. She did not remember meeting me. Perhaps I once accompanied my mother to this apartment and waited in that alcove during her hour. Perhaps I saw Menaker myself. At one point when my difficulties were getting out of hand in grade school, I was briefly referred to a play therapist—a woman—who talked with me while we involved ourselves in card and board games. One day, because I was in no mood to play, I took a deck of cards and flung them all over the room. The therapist reached over and slapped me across the face. At least I think she did. Could this therapist have been Menaker? It's possible. But it's also possible that the incident never happened, that I embellished it over the years from an acorn now forgotten—or even that I made the whole thing up. I was too embarrassed to mention any of this.

Menaker told me she had begun treating my mother in the early or mid-forties for depression. She was so depressed she initially needed support more than anything. "Analysis" at the outset seemed futile. In those days, Menaker said, she regularly met with a group of colleagues to discuss different cases, and she emphasized the work she had been doing with my mother because she knew her approach was atypical— and her colleagues, accordingly, criticized her sharply. But, she said, she was doing exactly what was most needed in this case, which was to offer all-out, unconditional support for a person whose view of herself had been shattered.

My mother's original complaint, Menaker explained, was my father's harsh and unjust treatment of me. She felt betrayed by it, she said. Her feeling for my father was therefore deeply divided, very difficult to explain. To illustrate her point, Menaker recalled that an uncle of hers had been the notorious Russian double agent Azev. This man had informed on dozens of radicals to the Czar's secret police in the years before the revolution. He was finally executed. The family had been disgraced and shamed by him. At a dinner at her father's house one night, Menaker recalled, Azev's son was present. What stuck in her mind was the look of disgust and longing on her father's face whenever he looked at his nephew. The sight of him made her father physically ill, but there was also such obvious tenderness and sorrow for the boy's loss, for what fate had done to him, that he became fascinated by him, without being able to open his heart to him. That was the kind of divided feeling, Menaker said, that she thought my mother had for my father.

She believed my mother was a confused person and that her confusion prevented her from seeing herself. Her *raison d'être*—quite sincere, she said—was identification with the unfortunate and with causes in their behalf. My mother identified with her parents and their circle, with the immigrants who had come here out of their different forms of hell only to face hard times once more. At the same time, my mother was just as sincerely a bohemian, a radical scorner of the very conventions and values cherished by those groups.

Who was the real person? Menaker did not know. She

said that it took my mother eight months to get around to revealing my birth story. It was only then that Van Heflin's name came up. He was someone my mother admired, looked up to as a kind of mentor in the theater, someone she was willing to be guided by, she said. She had passionate feelings for him and was unwilling to blame him for what had happened. Menaker told me my mother was unable to explain why it had taken her so long to mention any of that.

This only added to the puzzle of my mother's guilt, which, Menaker believed, was so deep and painful that she had devoted herself to evading it—hence her confusion. There was no point in trying to say what the sources of her guilt might have been—feeling for her parents, her dead sister, failing to live up to the rigid standards of her family, marrying someone she didn't love—so that in the end her guilt was as mysterious as it was pervasive. Menaker said she spent much time thinking about what it might have been like for a young woman to have wanted to go into the theater, to have been in a family that so valued learning, and then to have dropped out of school, seeking a life apart from convention, to have had a child out of wedlock, defying her family in order to hold on to it. She pointed out that the pseudonym Stone my mother used for herself when she had me was likely taken from a contemporary crusader for women's sexual freedom and reproductive rights, Lucy Stone.

Menaker remembered that my mother once turned up for an appointment with her hair out of place. "I remember your mother's words. 'It's a little wild—like me,'" Menaker said. "She had no one in her life who appreciated that."

While growing up, I always knew something was *off* about my mother, though I could not begin to say what. I could tell from the way she smoked cigarettes, for instance. She chain-smoked each cigarette down to the unfiltered tip between her yellowed fingers, dragging the smoke in with hard, almost angry inhalations of breath so you could see the smoke whip back into her mouth and down her throat. She constantly dropped long ashes onto table surfaces, floors, chairs, her own clothing. She always left burning butts on the edges of shelves, tables, countertops, so that all of them over time looked as though they had been worked over by a blow torch. My mother's illnesses, her cooking, even her first ludicrous attempts to drive a car seem in retrospect like clues.

I remember the day she tried to drive. We all nearly got killed. I was thirteen, and my father had just purchased a new gunmetal-colored Chevrolet sedan, which he was very proud of. We all piled into the car one Sunday afternoon and set out for the Concourse, to visit my grandparents. My father let my mother drive. He had been giving her lessons and had decided she was ready for her first big venture in traffic. With a flourish of warnings to us not to tease her, he slipped into the passenger seat next to her and we set off. The car had a stick shift, and every block or so my mother, who could not seem to coordinate the clutch, would buck the car until it stalled.

When we crossed the 207th Street bridge and headed up Fordham Road, traffic became heavier. At the Concourse, my mother made a wide, looping turn that nearly took out a line of pedestrians. She came bucking to a stop before she hit them. From the backseat, my brother and I whooped and carried on. My father turned and barked for us to be quiet. Then he swung his attention back to my mother and explained, very gently, about turns and smooth clutch control. She gave

him a vague look, but you could *feel* her attention riveted on
the road ahead. The strange thing was that she did not seem
to be afraid so much as angry. We came to a red light and
pulled to a bucking stop on the Concourse. My brother and I
this time made car sounds into our hands, which we had
pressed to our faces.

Then, when the light changed, my mother must have hit
the clutch, brake, and gas pedal all at the same time. The car
seemed to leap out of its frame, off its wheels, bucking and
heaving its way forward like a bull shot out of a holding pen.
My mother could not or would not take her foot off the gas
pedal. My father, all of us, yelled. He tried to get the steering
wheel from her. The car lurched forward, missing one vehicle
and a taxicab which swerved to avoid taking an almost broad-
side hit. One hundred, two hundred yards later, as we veered
all over the road, my mother took the car into the back of a
city bus.

Miraculously, no one was hurt and there was little damage to the car save for a flattening of the strong front guard
bumper. The bus driver and my father stood out on the street,
deciding that not enough harm had been done to hold up
traffic further. My mother meanwhile lit up a cigarette and
waited for my father to return to the car, almost as if she was
annoyed by the delay. When he got back, he asked her if she
would like to let him drive. No, she said, she was fine—and
we continued on our way, in silence, bucking all the way to
my grandparents' house.

I know now that I saw without seeing. What I knew was
that my mother lived in another world, though I could not
have begun to say what that world was. I also knew that there
was something not quite right between her and my father. It
was a mood, an attitude, a sensing of discomfort between

them. One of my earliest memories—maybe I was four—was of sneaking into my parents' bedroom on a Sunday morning, crawling underneath their bed, and just lying there, listening to them sleep. When we were living in Inwood, my father, after a drink or two, would sometimes put a Bing Crosby record on our new Webcor phonograph and want to dance with my mother. She would join him—briefly. But after a whirl or two around the foyer floor, she would disengage herself, saying, "That's enough, Ben," and she would retreat to the kitchen. My parents never went out much, never talked much in the living room after dinner.

I had a best friend in Inwood whose parents I wished were my own. They always seemed glad to see me. When they moved to New Jersey, I visited them there. The father or mother would come pick me up and drive me to their new house in Montclair, then back again after the weekends. The father would take my friend and me to the movies or to an ice-cream parlor, we would all play games in the backyard, and sometimes, in the evenings, both parents would dress up and take us to a restaurant or to the movies. The mother and father often held hands in the street. They would laugh and nuzzle affectionately. In the living room, after dinner, the mother would rest her head against the father's shoulder, while he had one arm spread out on the back of the sofa and the other around her, as we all listened to the radio. When they took me back on Sunday evenings, I went immediately to my room and closed the door so my parents would not see how unhappy I was at having to come home.

Secrecy in adoption is meant to protect people, not to hurt them. But what is protected is a lie, the fiction of a life with something fundamental missing—an authentic history. The effects of this on all involved are subtle but certain. "When there are secrets in a family system," writes Betty Jean Lifton in her book *Journey of the Adopted Self*, "there is a conspiracy of silence. The conspiracy does not have to be agreed upon verbally, but can be unconsciously communicated to members of a clan. A conspiracy holds family members together like a negative energy force, but it also keeps them apart. Stronger than any one individual, it controls whatever interactions take place. It feeds on the emotions of its victims like the Minotaur in the labyrinth: it demands tributes of loyalty and submission. Invisible as radiation, it can be lethal."

In my home, the effects of secrecy in our interactions were many-headed—a hydra, not a Minotaur. My mother could never show any of the conflicted and tumultuous feelings that she had gone to Esther Menaker with. She could never reveal to any of her children that her firstborn son had been the creation of a lost but still-cherished "wild" side of herself.

My father was as much controlled by *his* secret. My brother was really his firstborn son, but he was bound to hold back even the hint of the most natural and inescapable pride of blood he might have felt.

My brother, in his way, was as distorted by all of this as anyone. He was tuned to my father's rhythms—they were his—but he always believed I was the favorite, largely because of my father's efforts at disguise and my mother's not-so-careful willingness to tilt her feelings toward me. This tilting on my mother's part drove my brother to take his eye off her, so that he, like me, believed she was not the power in the family. There was around all of us—children, parents, grand-parents, aunts, uncles, cousins, friends-in-the-know—an air of fabricated authenticity that each of us, consciously or unconsciously, willingly supported.

Where this system broke down was in the interaction between my father and myself. I did poorly in school, flunking courses, getting into fights, bringing home report cards that were filled with notations about "conduct" problems and an unwillingness to "apply" myself. My father would constantly badger me to get homework done, to clean up my room first so that I would be able to find my books in the mess. He would confront me with how easy subjects like arithmetic were, and how easy it should have been for me to do well. He would take paper and pencil and impatiently show me how a problem was done, finishing it with a quick flourish of strokes, as though any fool should have been able to do it just as easily.

The older I got, the more trouble I seemed to attract. Increasingly, my father's responses to me were divided between outbursts of rage and icy disdain. Sometimes he would pass by me in a room or in a hallway and seem not to see me—as though, by some trick of conjuring, or by virtue of something I had done, I had become invisible.

I was now too tall to hit. But that created new and different levels of conflict. I began staying out late at night. I would hang out with friends, go to parties, sometimes wander over to Fordham Road with a couple of the older guys who swore it was easier to pick up girls in that part of the Bronx. One night I didn't get back until almost four in the morning. Where was I? my father asked harshly. Out, I said, walking past him to my room. My mother held him by the arm but told me the next day that he had been worried sick and had actually called the police to report a missing person. When he described me—six feet tall, 165 pounds—my mother said the police laughed and told him to go back to bed. There was a touch of amusement in her voice when she told me this, I thought, though she did then take pains to insist that in the future I had to let them know when I was going to be out past midnight.

By the time I reached the ninth grade, I was no longer in an academic program at school. I had flunked my way to days full of shop courses. I spent my time at Junior High School 52, learning how to use wood, electrical wiring, and sheet metal. The goal of the program was not really to teach skills but to keep the inmates occupied from nine to three. I remember bringing home a project from school one day, a rectangular block of wood, sanded, varnished to a shine. The sides of the block were erratically planed, supposedly to edges of forty-five degrees. The surface had eight holes, not so well spaced, and eight pegs that fit them, some tightly, some as loose as pencils in a cup. I gave it to my parents, announcing that it was a menorah. It disappeared within a day.

I did not finish the year at JHS 52. Midway through that fall, my parents decided that it would be better for me to go to boarding school. I am not sure whose idea it was to get me out of the house. I suspect it was my mother's, because my father could never have initiated a move like that. I can imagine that she had concluded there was really no other way to save me from myself, or from my father's fury. Accordingly, one day that fall, I was sent off to the Cherry Lawn School in Darien, Connecticut, a place that advertised itself as "a school not for problem children but a school for children with problems."

I had no way of knowing it at the time but, save for summers and a brief period in my early twenties, I would never again be a permanent resident in my parents' home.

FIVE

1.

I don't remember my leave-taking at all. Did my mother spend the day packing a trunk and labeling my clothing, did she make a fuss over what I was wearing, make sure that I had spending money in my pocket? Did she embrace me tightly before I left? Was my father there that day or was he at work? Where were my brother and sister? Were they peering out from behind my mother's skirts, wondering what was going on? I can answer none of these questions, because I remember nothing. Whatever I was feeling—abandonment, excitement, misery, adventure—none of it registered as we walked out the door, packed the car, and drove off.

What I do remember is that it was my uncle Morty, not

my parents, who took me to Darien. I also remember that it was late afternoon. I recall that because, when I finally dropped my things off at the dorm, it was dark out and Morty walked me into the school dining room, into a blaze of lights and the din of 120 students, eight to a table. None of them seemed distracted by the sight of a gaunt, well-dressed man and a boy walking up to the head table, which was presided over by the dean of students, a woman with a dyed, rust-colored hay-bale of a hairdo. I remember the way the light bounced off her eyeglasses, and her smile, wide as a barn. I remember feeling relief at seeing my uncle turn and go, leaving me there on my own.

I remember nothing about my early days at the school. I believe I got along with everyone—I certainly have no recollection of enemies or antagonists—but from day one, I simply could not bring myself to go to classes. I spent many of those early weeks alone in a gymnasium, shooting baskets, or just taking walks by myself, off the grounds of the school, up and down nearby roads, sometimes into Darien a mile and a half away, going to movies or into stores to see what I could shoplift.

I saw my parents often, I know that. They came to see me or I went to see them almost every weekend. I know there were Sundays when I was lying on my bed on the porch on the second floor and someone downstairs yelled, "Siff! Your parents!" But I can't say for sure that this ever actually happened. I can remember the taste of Cheddar-cheese soup at a restaurant my parents took me to on a Sunday afternoon. I can see the colonial look of the place, the dark interior, the heavy oak beams across the ceiling, the nooks and tables set with little brass candleholders, the waitresses wearing decorative linen aprons and tiny white dairy-maid bonnets—but I can't remember anything my parents said to me or I to them during four years of visits while I was in the Cherry Lawn School.

Much passed between us, I know. I came home for holidays, semester breaks, summers—and I was suspended from school three different times. Once, I was caught in the girls' dorm, my thirteen-year-old girlfriend and I half undressed; another time, I was packed off for breaking and entering the school kitchen after hours and stealing a large cooked roast beef and a five-gallon can of ice cream. I was filled with the spirit of Pretty Boy Floyd: I wanted every poor kid on my floor to eat well and be happy. The third time, I got into a fight with a teacher, an assistant football coach named Mr. Wright, whom everyone called "Never." Never accused me of being cowardly during a football game as we were heading out of the dorm on our way to the dining hall. I grabbed him by the collar, pushed him against a wall, and made a fist, which I swung toward his face, stopping an inch short of it as I kicked the plasterboard wall behind him, hoping the sound would scare him to death. Instead, my foot went through the wall. I don't think I would have been suspended but for the property destruction that was involved; in any case, I was homeward bound once more. I have no memory whatever of my parents' reactions to any of these unwelcome visitations.

The sense of detachment or numbness I developed around my parents over the years has seemed peculiar to me. I am more inclined now to believe it had not so much to do with separating from them as a teenager as with the first separation itself, what I learned and didn't learn when my mother gave me up right after I was born.

Contemporary writing on adoption is rife with the term "attachment theory." Different experts have different views of its effects, but there is unanimous agreement that an early rupturing of the bond—or attachment—between mother and child has certain consequences. Most writing focuses on the damage to children. Feminists and others make strong arguments that "attachment theory" is exaggerated and serves only to bind women to the home. But the most widely held view comes from the British psychiatrist John Bowlby, who, along with French psychiatrist René Spitz, did a series of studies in the 1940s and '50s on the effects of separating children from their mothers. Bowlby concluded that an early severing of the bonds had measurable and specific consequences later on. In a recent article on attachment theory, Margaret Talbot summarized Bowlby's research: "In all of [the] cases, Bowlby detected an initial stage of protest, followed by a kind of passive grief or dejection that could sometimes appear to be cooperative behavior . . . followed by a deeper and more lasting emotional detachment—the child might be cheerful with others, but defensively reject his mother when she appeared again."

Talbot points out that for decades now researchers have been striving to add flesh to the bones of Bowlby's and Spitz's work, seeking to demonstrate conclusively the particular ways in which severed attachment has an impact on children. A classic experiment in the field, Talbot notes, is "a miniature melodrama known as the Strange Situation." In the experiment, researchers place themselves behind two-way mirrors; a twelve-month-old child is then brought into a room filled with toys by its mother (very infrequently by its father), and then, for two brief periods in the next twenty minutes, the mother leaves the child, once with a researcher, once alone. The child's reactions are observed. "What matters most, according to the logic of the Strange Situation," Talbot writes,

> is not what happens in the separations but what happens in the reunions. If the baby is upset, as most are, when his mother leaves him in this strange place, but if he also seeks comfort from her when she returns, then he is considered securely attached. If he isn't particularly upset, but still pads over to her or looks up at her and smiles when she comes back into the room, then he is considered secure, too. Insecure children, on the other hand, fall into two main categories. The "avoidant" types scarcely seem to notice their mother when she's in the room, show few overt signs of distress when she leaves it and mostly ignore her when she returns. And the "ambivalent" types often wail inconsolably when she leaves—but are not pacified by her return.

The observations drawn from this and other data strongly suggest, in Talbot's words, "that there is evidence that the categories of attachment—secure and insecure—tend to persist and to shape the personalities of older children and young adults."

According to this research, I was an "avoidant" type. If this is so, I must, early on, have developed that peculiar kind of numbness whereby, no matter how much fuss and bother was made by my mother, no matter what *she* felt, I remained largely oblivious, secure not in any feeling relationship I had with her but in the *absence* of feeling.

To be sure, I did have a sense of my home and the people in it during the years I spent at boarding school. But I felt like a distant observer, taking in what happened as if it were not part of my life, as though I were standing outside and looking through the living-room window.

My mother was fretful and constantly worried. Her manner was, as usual, dramatic and exaggerated, but it seemed she had much to be concerned about. My sister, Judy, almost nine years younger than me, worried her. She had epilepsy—like Nancy—and both my parents hovered around her. One day, my father fell ill with a bleeding ulcer. I was home on a break (or was it summer? I forget) when this happened. He was rushed to the hospital, where three-quarters of his stomach was removed and the remaining part was resectioned. Though of course frightened, I was more aware of my mother's fear, her grim manner. In the end, there was only a storm of feeling, high black clouds over the entire family but off at a distance from my life.

My father's illness galvanized my mother. A caretaker, she became obsessed with having to tend to him, a daunting task. His first and most irreducible need, she knew, was psychotherapy, to relieve the pressure cooker that had steamed his stomach into ulcers. But when he objected to that, she let Esther Menaker lead her to an alternative. Menaker knew an Austrian painter named Trude Waehner who happened to live in my parents' neighborhood. She knew Trude from her time in Vienna, training as an analyst with Anna Freud. Trude had the necessary bona fides—politically progressive, bohemian in her lifestyle, devoted to her art. My mother first got my father to express a willingness to try drawing and painting. She went out and bought him supplies—a pad, some sticks of charcoal, a bottle of fixative, brushes, and a few tubes of paint. She lavishly praised his initial efforts. Then she invited Trude over to dinner.

When I came home periodically from Cherry Lawn, I found new paintings in frames on the walls or stacked away in closets. Our house seemed to acquire a permanent odor of turpentine and linseed oil. My father painted with zeal if not with inspiration or draftsmanship. He seemed drunk on French impressionism. Sunlight and tiers of heaving blue-shadowed leaves, bright grasses, dark clumps of woods, and little mottled shacks on country lanes were his favorite subjects—all from Inwood Hill Park or from obscure wooded corners of nearby Riverdale. His portraits were careful, colorful, workmanlike, and inaccurate. There was one of my brother, cross-eyed and lopsided—the closest he ever came to a likeness—reading a Looney Tunes comic book; there was another of my mother which somehow made her look like Claudette Colbert with two black eyes and a long history of opium addiction.

Nothing seemed more important than my father's painting. Perhaps because I spent so much time away, I was more struck by this than I might have been. Everything seemed given over to his new passion. On Saturday mornings, he took his lessons with Trude. Eventually, because of his enthusiasm—or my mother's—my uncle Morty took up painting as well, as did my mother's old YPSL comrade and neighbor, Max Rosenberg, and my sister. With the exception of Judy, who actually became a serious painter, none of the other students lasted beyond that first wave of enthusiasm, but Saturday mornings at Trude's must have seemed like Oil Painting I at Cooper Union. When summers came and my parents packed for vacation, the car was piled with rolls of canvas, wood for frames, easels, glue, paint boxes, sketch pads—to the point where some household essentials might have been left behind. My father dressed differently. He had a ragged straw hat and he wore paint-splattered pants and had a fondness for shirts with ripped sleeves opened to the middle of the chest. My parents chose vacation spots for their subject attractiveness: an island lodge on Lake Magaguadavic, in the wilds of the Maritime Provinces; a farmhouse on a hill in Dutchess County; and, of course, Trude's home in the south of France.

Without realizing it, I measured what was going on in my family, the underlying mood, by my father's paintings—and I did this to the day he died. When I came home from school, I always had a reaction to the new paintings I saw, whether or not I thought they were good. There was one of my sister and her friend Ellie, Max Rosenberg's daughter, sitting on a beach looking out at the water. The style of the painting was simple: flat planes, few details, solid colors. The mood was sunny and uncomplicated—happy. Another painting on the wall, done in France, was a landscape of a farmhouse set against the backdrop of a large, perfectly rounded hill. Sunlight floods the scene, but it is hard to imagine anyone working in the fields or going in and out of that farmhouse. The feeling in the painting, without the hustle and bustle of human life, is perfectly serene.

What I now know is that, just because my eye was so riveted on my father as a Sunday painter, I gradually lost sight of my mother in those years. She seemed settled in her routine as a "homemaker." She did what she always did around the house, the only variation, perhaps, an earlier start to cocktail hour. Rosenberg's wife, Isabel, joined her, as did Harriet and a couple of women from the neighborhood, including her old YPSL friend Florence Rossi. These women were noisy and friendly. "Boozeday Tuesday" was the term my mother used many years later to describe an afternoon at Florence's, though Rossi used to refer to my mother as "the Champ" when it came to drinking. When I was around, I enjoyed these women because I could perform for them.

The army-McCarthy hearings were being televised then, and I was able to imitate all of the principal players, including Tail Gunner Joe, Roy Cohn, G. David Schine, and Everett Dirksen. The women encouraged me and tried to get me to drink with them, though I knew I was always at an advantage if I kept myself sober.

I would not have known anything was different in my mother's life, still less what she might then have been thinking and feeling about herself, if she had not decided, seemingly out of the blue, to get her high-school equivalency so she could go on to college. While I was at Cherry Lawn, she began taking degree courses at Columbia's School of General Studies. She remained at General Studies for the next seven years, until she got a bachelor's degree and then a master's. This decision of hers to pursue her education allowed me, ironically, to begin to see a side of her that I believe she wanted to keep hidden. I could make only limited sense of this at the time, but it was enough to make me aware that she was not quite who I thought she was.

2.

It was not clear that my mother began with more than a simple desire to earn a degree. She had no plans to teach, for example, or to use whatever degree she got for a job or for a career. Esther Menaker believed her purpose in going to school was related to her own starved intellectual curiosity, and to an even deeper need to make herself feel better about who she was. But there was more to it than that.

She was a student with a vengeance. She loved preparing for classes. She stayed up late at night and on weekends working on her assignments. Her professors—Mark Van Doren and Lionel Trilling—became heroes. This was especially so because it was the age of red-baiting, and in my mother's mind a lecture on Shakespeare or on the liberal imagination inevitably became a kind of regal assault on McCarthyism that went far beyond the perishable complaints of editorialists and journalists.

My mother was one of a handful of students selected for a weekly televised sunrise semester of a General Studies course on the Great Books of Western Civilization. As I was away at school, and because there was no videotaping then and kinescopes from that era were not preserved, I saw her only once or twice on this program. She sat at a round table with seven or eight other students. The background was dark, the overhead lighting severe, there was a ring of faces caught starkly in white light threaded by rising columns of cigarette smoke. I remember nothing about the program itself other than its ambience and the intent look on my mother's face.

My mother never seemed too taken with herself for being on television. If anything, she downplayed her appearances, as though they were really incidental to going to school and taking courses. But I never entirely believed this, because I knew that throughout her life she was vain about her looks, certain that her nose, perfectly small and straight, was too thick, her jaw too wide, her face too fat. How could she have gone on television without worrying about how she looked?

But there was no question that she was completely absorbed in her coursework. Textbooks, library books, note-books, course papers proliferated in our house, alongside my father's paintings. From day to day, my mother's energies were clearly devoted to school, try as she did to keep up with the routines of housework. There were any number of evenings when she disappeared after dinner, leaving the dishes and the kitchen to others.

My father tried to be her cop and business manager. He was the one who demanded quiet so she could work unhindered in the living room during the evenings. Sometimes he would take us out in the car to a local ice-cream parlor or, once or twice, to a movie so my mother would have the advantage of peace and quiet while she worked on her term papers.

I vaguely remember one she did about Babbitt and Oblomov, a typical piece of lit crit comparing and contrasting characters who seemingly had little in common. There was a longer paper, her master's thesis, which I recall more clearly, perhaps because my mother was proudest of it, but also because it changed the way I thought about her. The paper, called "The Angry Young Women," was about the Brontës, mainly about the life and work of Charlotte Brontë.

My mother saw Charlotte as a shy and buried person, caught in terrible circumstances but on fire with ambition— and anger. From the time of her childhood, Charlotte lived in her imagination, created a whole world of imaginary characters and stories, a kingdom she called "Angria." In this kingdom, there were rivalries, jealousies, plots, counterplots, machinations that always seemed to lead inevitably to the injuring of a young girl's spirit. Everywhere she went, in everything she did, there was a burden of expectation, which, by choice, she shouldered without complaint. But anger, fury, longing consumed her. She wrote in secret, her mind a storm of dreams, images, ideas against which her plain day-to-day life formed a kind of curious façade, protecting her, hiding her from a world which remained unaware of her gifts. In her anonymity, she was finally able to speak to the world, teasing it, surprising it with mastery. She was both ravaged and inspired by her gifts. Illness, poverty, alcohol, madness, longing were part of the bleak landscape of the moors that surrounded her and fueled her imagination.

My mother's picture of Charlotte reminded me a little too much of herself. Charlotte, like her, had two sisters, one of whom she loved and jealously resented, the other of whom she had a tendency to look down on. She was devoted to her family but resentful and jealous of them, too. The pressure of keeping things hidden made her angrier and angrier (at least that was how I read it at the time). But Charlotte was terribly shy and was unable to show this side of herself to anyone. As my mother presented her, if Charlotte had lived in America in the 1950s, she might well have been a frustrated Bronx housewife.

It was a revelation to think about my mother as one of the

Brontës. Though this didn't last long, it was the earliest glimpse I had of her buried, secret life. That I misinterpreted it seems beside the point now. I focused on my mother's anger because, at the time, that was what made the most sense to me. I was able to step back from my usual vantage point, from which I saw her as soft-hearted and soft-headed, to see someone very different. I couldn't begin to see the whole of her life or all that she might have been hiding, but I was able to see her anger. I was able to see it day to day, and I was able to look back, to see it in her past and realize that it had probably always been there.

3.

Once, when I was home for Passover, we went to my grandparents' for the seder. The usual roundup of relatives was there: Lee and Docky, Harriet and Morty and their children, my parents, my brother, sister, and I, a homely cousin from Queens who liked boys and syrupy Manischewitz wine. But the star attractions that night were Harold's sister Hilda and her husband, Lou, a struggling screenwriter, émigrés from California, where, they said, they had been victimized by the Hollywood blacklist (something my mother doubted: "Lou *polishes* scripts," she said at the time, "he doesn't *sell* them").

Hilda and my mother had a long history of rivalry and jealousy. Hilda was a petite, attractive woman, slightly built, with long, thick, rust-colored hair wound tightly in a braid and pinned at the top of her head. She had sparkling green eyes, a ready smile, and a throaty voice as deep as Tallulah

Bankhead's but without a hint of sarcasm. From the time she was a young girl, she was a flirt and a siren. The young men in the family were blinded by her. They pursued her like victims of the Sirens or, rather, she went for them, especially if they were already spoken for. Morty, for example, after he had begun dating Harriet, had had his head turned by the radiant Hilda. For a while, he was one of a number of "respectable" boyfriends Hilda collected and brought home to her red household. All these boys had good jobs on Wall Street. They turned up "very nattily dressed," Harold remembered. "They all wore black coats and velvet collars." The unimpressed patriarchs of the family—Hilda and Harold's father, Beryl, and my grandfather—snickeringly referred to these boys as "the Derbies."

But Hilda's biggest sin was that she cut into my mother's territory. She was not particularly interested in school, though she did go to college. She was interested in dance and theater—as well as boys. My mother and Harold especially resented her because she was older—Harriet's age—and seemed to maintain a carefree nature free of any major difficulties or complications. In my mother's mind, Hilda was never serious about anything she did. Actress? She was never more than a member of a chorus of rabbits in a play about beavers that had a one-night stand under the auspices of the WPA. Dancer? Where? At summer camp? Radical? Hilda went to bed with them, she wasn't one herself.

In any case, at the seder that night, after everyone had assembled at the long table in my grandparents' living room, the table splendidly set with its rows of Lee's finest bone-china plates, the gleaming monogrammed Segal cutlery, the fresh vases of flowers and dark stalks of newly lighted can-

dles, some time between the placing of the first serving of
gefilte fish and the evening's first prayer from Docky, my
mother, scurrying back and forth with plates from the
kitchen, got into some sort of quarrel with Hilda. My mother
said later it was about politics, of course, but who knew. As
the women were moving from kitchen to living room, I
remember first hearing Hilda's Tallulah Bankhead voice rising, saying, "Don't be an idiot! Don't be an idiot!" My
mother's voice: "Who are you calling an idiot?" "Oh, Eleanor,
shut up!" "*Shut UP?* How dare you!" "Oh, please, *please!*" It was
the loudness of their voices more than anything they were
saying that suddenly quieted everyone else in the room. My
mother and Hilda kept at it like a pair of macaws, until my
mother veered toward the table, slammed a pair of silver serving spoons down loud as a gunshot, turned, and, with her face
literally inches from Hilda's, roared, "*Did you ever consider the
possibility that just once you might be wrong?*"

My mother, short as she was, looked like Hippolyta,
Queen of the Amazons, towering over Hilda, whose frozen
face, tilting upward, had suddenly become a raspberry pop.
Just like that, she uttered a short, incoherent cry and fled the
room in tears. Lou, Docky, and my father were on their feet.
Then Lee and Lou were in pursuit of Hilda; my father, Docky,
and now Harriet were at my mother's side, trying to lead her
by the arm to a place at the table.

"Eleanor, for God's sakes, it's Pesach!" Harriet urgently
whispered.

"Shut the fuck up!" my mother snarled, elbowing herself
free, then dropping herself into a chair, where she snapped
open a napkin, placed it on her lap, and immediately took a
gulp of the not-yet-blessed wine from the cut-crystal goblet
at her place setting.

There was also the time my grandfather was hospitalized with a stroke. I was home from school on vacation and went to visit him at his bedside with my brother and sister. I remember him sitting in a chair in his bathrobe, blue pajamas, and slippers. His hair had been plastered back in a thin greasy sheet. His glasses gleamed on his nose, one eye looking bigger than the other. He grinned when he saw us, part of his mouth going up one side of his face, the rest of his mouth looking as if it were nailed to his gums. My mother and grandmother were a pair of Swiss Guards around the Pope's throne when we entered the room. I remember little more of the day than this snapshot, but I remember the days before and after, when my mother hurriedly left the house in the morning, irritable and uncommunicative, not returning again until well after we had dined that evening on dishes of nearly indigestible food she had prepared earlier.

She was in constant turmoil over the care my grandfather was or wasn't receiving at the hospital—the slowness of nurses in answering call bells, neglect in housekeeping, in bringing medicines to him on time, in getting him up to walk or to go to the bathroom, above all in their manner of talking to him, which my mother believed was condescending and insulting. She badgered my father to take action against the hospital, to threaten them with the filing of an official complaint or even a lawsuit. She would rasp about this doctor or that administrator. She would rattle ice cubes around in her glass of scotch, drag hard on her cigarette, and begin muttering imprecations, almost to herself, directed at doctors who had become so self-important they had forgotten how to deal with human beings.

My grandfather died and my grandmother moved in with us. We relocated to Riverdale from Inwood, into a larger, sunnier apartment. But my mother's mood noticeably darkened. It was hard to tell whether this was because she had someone looking over her shoulder telling her what to do, or for some other reason. But she was frequently out of sorts, and from time to time she would snap at my grandmother, something I had never seen her do before.

And then there was my father's father, Grandpa Grischa. Not long after my mother's father died and my grandmother began living with us, she had to deal with him one summer in her own expanded Kingdom of Angria.

4.

By then, I was a year out of prep school (I had done just enough to pass my courses and graduate). That summer, just before my sophomore year in college, my parents rented a farmhouse in Dutchess County, a brown-shingled rectangle of a building on top of a hill, with a pond down below and a long view of a valley and the Catskill Mountains. It was a perfect place for painting and writing. My father went out in the fields with his straw hat, easel, and folding stool early in the morning, and he would sit through the day as if he were Gauguin in Brittany. My mother spent her mornings on the screened-in front porch, reading or writing down "ideas" in a notebook which she carried around with her.

All of this stopped when the furious Dr. Ziev had a heart attack and came to the country to recuperate with us. My mother could barely bring herself to stay in the same room with him. The doctor was ashen-faced, moody, and largely content to sit through entire days on the front porch fanning himself and staring into space with a strange smile on his face that reminded me a little of Groucho Marx in the years after he had his stroke. In the afternoons, my mother rounded up my brother, my sister, and me and got us to go down to the pond, where she sat against a canvas sling-back, smoking, doing crossword puzzles, occasionally slipping into the water for a minute or two of gentle dog-paddling. My father never accompanied us. He stayed behind in the house to be with his father, and with my grandmother, who did not like to take the sun.

I was always curious about my father's father, probably because I spent so little time with him. I had all kinds of romantic notions about his having been a Russian revolutionary. I constantly asked questions about him, enough to know that my mother was not the person to go to if I wanted my curiosity satisfied. Her stories about him were one-sided and always familiar. She would reiterate that my father had been forced to speak Russian while growing up in the United States, because his father insisted they would be going back to Russia after the revolution—which, of course, they did, at the point when my father had finally become assimilated. She was the one who made us aware that my father, at seventeen, was so alienated that he almost ran away from home.

Obviously, I knew nothing about what might have been behind my mother's ill-will toward my grandfather, the feelings of anger, shame, and unworthiness he had provoked in her. What I did know was that the air was heavy in the house whenever they got together.

Grandpa Grischa stayed with us for two weeks—more time in proximity than in all the years of my parents' marriage put together. My father's forays into the fields were curtailed as he stayed behind with his father for long hours during the days, going over different legal papers or just being there to keep him company. My mother's notebook seemed to vanish completely. I tried to engage my grandfather in conversation—not very successfully. I'd ask him to tell me how he had met my grandmother in Siberia when they were both political prisoners, or how he had come to meet Trotsky. He would always act as though he couldn't understand my English, and I never pressed him. I knew he didn't really like to talk.

One evening, after dinner, I got him to play chess with me. This was something of a coup. He was reluctant to play with me, because he was really good and knew it. He belonged to a family of chess players, one of whom—a nephew, I think—was a grand master. We sat on the porch after dinner and I set up the pieces on a board before us after he told me to play whatever color I chose. I beat him—and in not too many moves. I remember that afterward I was very pleased with myself, and worried about my grandfather, too, thinking he might have lost because he was sick. But he seemed pleased for me. "Good boy," he said, "good boy." It was as if I had made it through a rite of passage and I was now welcomed into the long line of chess-playing Siffs. I went inside for some reason, I don't remember why, and my mother collared me and asked me to help bring out serving trays of tea, coffee, and cake to the porch.

Just as my mother and I were approaching the doorway to the porch, we heard my grandfather saying something to my father in a broken voice. Both my mother and I stopped, not wanting to intrude. The old man said: "Ben, I think I'm losing my mind!" My father answered: "Why do you think that?"

"*David* beat me in chess!" he said.

A peculiar smile drifted over my mother's face. She nudged me forward. "Tea? Coffee?" she said in a melodious voice, striding out onto the porch.

When my father finally drove my grandfather back to the Bronx, my parents barely seemed to be speaking to each other. By the time my father got back that night, we had already eaten. My mother looked up from a book she was reading in the living room, asked how his father fared on the trip home, told my father there was food for him in the refrigerator if he wanted it. She did not get up to join him.

The next day, my father and brother suddenly got into a fight. The two of them were caught on a balcony level that stretched from one end of the house to the other. Who knows what their fight was about. The real combatants were my parents.

My mother, sitting in the living room below, was on her feet instantly. I remember staying in place as she whizzed past me. I had never seen her move so fast. She reached the two of them and flung herself at my father, trying to push him back. My brother was screaming, "*Go on, hit me! Hit me!*" I got to my feet and began moving, hesitantly, toward the stairs. But then, just like that—I don't know what my mother said, what she did—my father went limp. He just stood there, with my brother still screaming in his face. My mother walked my father a couple of steps down the hall and let him go; he kept on, moving almost like a somnambulist, until he reached the end of the balcony and the door of the bedroom he and my mother shared. He opened it, went inside, and closed the door behind him. My brother was still bellowing in the middle of the balcony. My mother simply stood in front of him like a boulder in a roadway until he finally subsided.

For the remainder of the time we spent there, my parents seemed to come and go as separate people in the same house. By then, I had come to understand that my mother was at the center of everything that went on in our family. It was her temperament—her temper—her needs and aspirations, never voiced, always present, that defined all our lives.

Now, decades later, I know that that time was crucial in her mind. She had just finished school, had submitted her thesis, gotten her degree. There was no discussion—at least none that took place within earshot of any of her children—about what all of that meant in her life. But I think the meaning of it dominated our home, something that had been awakened during my mother's years in school. What that was, precisely, I would not discover until long after her death—though her thesis on the Brontës had given me a clue.

All through her time in school, my father had been generous, supportive, and encouraging. He was also privy to what her friends, her children, and other relatives were not: he knew what had been stirred in her. And I believe it might have provoked him.

A painting from that period hints at this, a nighttime cityscape of Riverdale done from the window of our new apartment. The canvas looks out across a series of rooftops. The buildings, done in smoky, almost sulfuric hues, are crowded in upon one another, as though walls have become spines, the buildings leaning, almost clawing at each other for space. There are hundreds of windows, all of them lit, blazing like little spearpoints of fire in the night. The sky above is dramatically roiled by quilted clouds shot through from the glow of the city below. The color scheme throughout is obvious, the design of angles and planes of the different buildings even more so. The painting, devoid of a single human figure, is full of intense feeling. There is a furnace of anger and frustration in it; the walls of the bending buildings look as though they are about to explode.

But the explosion, somehow, never came.

SIX

1.

During my darkest days at Cherry Lawn, when I was flunking all my courses, I got the lead in a school play. The play was Terence Rattigan's *The Browning Version* and I played the part of the sad professor, at the end of his teaching career, caught in a barren marriage with a woman about to leave him. I was surprised to get the part. The director was Mr. Burwell, my English teacher, who had a somewhat negative view of me. I consistently flunked his courses and, on one occasion, when we were assigned *Ethan Frome*, a friend of mine and I got into a friendly contest—wagered upon by a circle of cheering classmates, but also observed by Mr. Burwell—to see who could break the book in half with his bare hands.

I remember feeling extremely jumpy before the play began. Backstage, I could hear the surf sounds of the audience in the gymnasium. I couldn't help myself. I went to the curtain, parted it just an inch or so, and peeked out. The place was filling up. There were friends, teachers—and my parents in one of the rows of metal folding chairs, about a third of the way back. My father was in a business suit, with a manila folder on his lap along with his hat. My mother was in a dark dress with a bright necklace. She had her arms folded, one under the other, one hand cupped under her chin, a forefinger resting thoughtfully alongside her nose. She was staring straight ahead. I quickly shut the folds of the curtain.

When the play began and I made my entrance, my hands were trembling so uncontrollably I had to shove them in my pockets. To the audience it must have been an odd gesture, given that my character was supposed to be ramrod formal. All I could think of was that I would drop any prop I handled, and that I would forget my lines. A diabolical force controlled me from a hidden panel of switches and dials. Before I said anything, I recited the upcoming line in my head to be sure I knew it. After a minute or so, once I had delivered a few lines on cue, my hands came out of my pockets, my limbs began to loosen, and I was no longer Frankenstein's monster. I began to sense the audience out in the darkness, could feel them, almost as another character in the play. My focus remained riveted on what I had to do onstage, but I became increasingly fascinated with this sense of connection I had with the crowd-animal, as though what I did could stroke them, soothe them, cajole them. At the end, standing on the stage for my curtain call, I was bathed in sweat and drunk with classmates chanting, "Siff! Siff! Siff!"

Triumph is blinding. How could I see that I really was just

a fifteen-year-old boy with a put-on British accent, stage silver in his hair, ludicrous amounts of makeup on his face, playing an arid middle-aged cuckold? I felt like Clark Gable in *Gone With the Wind*. My teachers were ecstatic about my performance. My parents were present as bystanders, witnesses to a miracle.

"You never told us he was an actor," one teacher gushed to them.

"He's a born actor. Did you know that?" Mr. Burwell said.

"Now we know!" another teacher said.

My parents smiled. My mother kissed me. "You were wonderful, darling," she whispered, as a way of letting me know—I thought then—that, beyond the bluster of my teachers, she really did think I was good.

I cannot imagine now what that evening must have been like for my parents, what they thought to themselves driving home that night, whether they connected what I had done in any way with my birth father, whose height I was, whose hands and high forehead I possessed, whose blood ran in my veins. When I think of them driving back down the Merritt Parkway, I can see my father with his eyes on the road, the shadows of trees on either side of the road, clumps of dark blurring against dark, my mother slouched in the corner of the passenger seat, working on her cigarette. There is music on the car radio, the glow of the radio dial on their faces. By the time they get to the Greenwich toll plaza, the New York stations are loud and clear, they are tuned in to *Fleetwood* or *Listening with Watson*. Perhaps my father says something about the divinity of Horowitz or Rubinstein—but I cannot imagine conversation between them in which Van Heflin's name would be mentioned, or in which either of them suggests that there is anything strange or out of the ordinary about seeing me onstage. My mother lets herself say aloud that I have always been a ham, and remembers how, when I was barely three, they took me to see *The Wizard of Oz* at Bronx Paradise Theater and then, afterward, because I remembered the words to the songs, they made a record of me singing. This is a moment of ordinary nostalgia. She parenthetically wonders if they still have the record somewhere. My father is sure they do, possibly in among the old photographs in a carton in the hall closet. After a while, perhaps repeating herself, my mother sighs and says how good it was to see me looking so happy. My father agrees.

I was in a couple of other plays at Cherry Lawn. I had a small part in *The Tempest*, and then I had a lead in the senior play, Lorca's *Blood Wedding*, which I quit because it got in the way of baseball practice. I also acted in college. I was Orsino in *Twelfth Night*, a production my mother hated because it was so stylized. Every move, every gesture was broad and exaggerated. In my opening monologue, "If music be the food of love . . . ," I blubbered, plastering the back of my hand to my forehead, sucking in big gulps of air as I reached a paroxysm of dandified grief. "Give me excess of it, that, surfeiting, / The appetite may sicken and so die. / That strain again! it had a dying fall. . . ." As I inhaled, I also happened to suck in my false beard, nearly choking to death onstage. My parents were in the audience. But what a trooper I had become by then. They, along with everyone else in the audience, could not see that I was in danger of asphyxiating; I gasped and wheezed and carried on—in the stylized manner of the production—concealing my heroic fight for life. When I got to the wings, I coughed and the scalding clot of beard popped loose and I was able to breathe again.

Perhaps because I had not only given a performance but

had also come close to making the ultimate sacrifice for my art, I anticipated great praise from my parents. What I got, instead, was an impolite, unalloyed, and withering blast from my mother, who said she hated our production and hated me in it for being so phony. I could not even begin to tell her what had happened.

We were standing outside the theater, a beautiful old converted carriage house in the woods, with scores of people around. My mother railed and carried on like Duse herself. She mockingly imitated me, throwing the back of her hand up to her head—grief; clapping both hands over her heart with a loud thump—surprise. How could I have been so false? she wanted to know. And, not waiting or willing to hear an answer, she provided one of her own. "I know it's not your fault, sweetheart, but the director should be shot."

What had I touched in my mother? She was normally so uncritical I discounted anything she said. She had praised me inordinately in all of the school productions in which she saw me. I can see myself as the prospector in Giraudoux's *Madwoman of Chaillot*, my nose in the air, a hand flamboyantly describing imaginary realms of capitalist conquest—wacko malarkey—and my mother greeting me afterward, almost in tears. Ditto for my playing Sam in Elmer Rice's *Street Scene*, a lothario in Schnitzler's *La Ronde*, a soul-sick knight errant in *Undine*.

What was so special about *Twelfth Night*? Could it have been that Viola—a young woman deprived and in disguise, who, in the name of love and sacrifice, endures calamities of indifference, misunderstanding, even abuse, only to be rescued in the bright blaze of truth, in the surrendering of all disguises to claim the ultimate reward of her heart's desire—

was a heroine too sublime to be poked fun at? Or was it that Orsino, the powerful Duke, blind to his own heart and to the woman who loves him, was a special type of man, never to be punctured with caricature?

Maybe my mother just didn't like what she saw, maybe she was out of sorts because Gristede's sent the wrong order that day. Still, *Twelfth Night* was special in the sense that it was the first school play I performed in that made me think about becoming a professional actor. Perhaps my mother sensed that, and feared I would never measure up if I showed myself in that way.

Something happened to me in that production. Until then, acting had always been a kind of lark and a safety valve, something I knew I could do when I was having a hard time doing much else. I did not major in drama in school. I never took an acting class. I was never part of the clique of "theater people" on campus. I realized, in doing this particular play, how much at home I felt on the stage. The feeling was eerie, almost mystical. I told my parents about it. When they asked how rehearsals were going, I told them I was enjoying myself so much I thought I might have found my calling. Did my mother see what I couldn't have seen, that there was an invisible hand beckoning to me from the wings?

When I graduated, I told myself I needed to do something more serious than acting. I went to the University of Iowa, intending to get a master's degree. I took courses, doing odd jobs to pay my way. I bussed tables in a fraternity, I modeled for an art class. I had a friend in Iowa City who had directed me in some plays over one summer at a resort in New Hampshire. He was getting a degree in theater arts, and I remember sitting with him one day listening to him lacerate me for not really being as serious as I said I wanted to be. If I was serious, why wasn't I an actor in New York or California? What was I doing in Iowa City?

Good question. I think I was there to please my parents but, four decades later, I can't even say that for sure. The only sign of seriousness about me then was the absence of fun in my life. My classes were uninteresting. My different jobs were tiring. One morning in the art class, I disrobed, took my position, and held it for a while—until I felt a tingling sensation in my legs. The sensation turned into a rush up my legs, into my torso. I was faint and had to break my pose and sit. Someone covered me with a sheet of cheesecloth as I sat on my stool. I had forgotten to eat.

I lost my wallet in Iowa City. I tracked a movie-theater janitor who I hoped might have found it down to where he lived, in a place called the Jefferson Hotel. With the chain on his door, he told me he didn't know anything about a wallet, but if I went back to the theater and asked the night manager to look on the lower shelf of the medicine chest in the maintenance closet, maybe I'd find it. It was there, money gone, cards intact, a message printed in a spidery hand on a piece of torn brown paper stuffed into the empty bill compartment: "You are missing something in your life," the oracle said.

I kept a journal then. The pages are full of my misadventures with women, candlelight dinners, quarrels, charades of wounded pride, jealousy, and longing. I could not bear to look at my own loneliness, yet I could write about nothing else. This boy in Iowa, poor fellow, trying to keep such a brave front in the face of his own misery—he goes to a concert of Beethoven chamber music, or an exhibition of the lithographer Mauricio Lasansky, and all he is thinking about is that he has no girlfriend. He comes to his rented attic apartment, foul-smelling with gas, feeds a stray kitten he has taken in off the street and whom he has named, after Dostoevsky, Stinking Lizaveta, because the poor animal is unable to be housebroken and constantly yowls for milk.

He cannot bear to come to grips with this loneliness. He confesses the Seven Deadly Sins to himself on a daily basis, sloth of sleeping, lusts of looking, pride of pretending, anger at everything. He says he is going back to New York to be an actor, but he has no idea what he is talking about. He is invested in being exhilarated, if only to keep himself from thinking that he is running away from something. In the manner of a twenty-two-year-old graduate student who has recently been reading Whitman, he takes out his journal on the train home and writes:

> . . . And Indiana and Ohio, the tankstops and the lightowers and the freightyards and eerie glow of strange towns, lost places. Farmland more farmland in the dawn's early light fog on the fields not pretty but like after a war or a storm branches shacks fields stripped bare dripping nobody moving there at all earth a gutted shell for awhile I'm the gutted shell. Freight train freight train going so far blur by shock of concussion the other way to Chicago or maybe further west, a yard a light, a watertower another factory. Who knows what I'm bringing back that I didn't have months before but I'll be damned if it's all for nada: twenty-two is a great age to be alive.

When I got to New York, my parents were waiting for me at the train station. I have no memory of this, but my journal says they were there. I take it as a given that, before we got from the concourse of the station to the street outside, I was blabbing on about my plans to be an actor, which I may or may not have mentioned on the phone when I told them I was coming home. I have no idea how my parents took the news. My mind, my journal are blank.

I hadn't a clue as to how to go about being an actor in New York. I woke up the first morning I was home and had a cold. I stayed put for three days. It is obvious now that I was meant to have that cold. On the fourth day (rather than the first, second, or third), I picked up the *New York Times* and read the want ads. There was a listing for a part-time yeshiva teacher in Brooklyn. I answered it. The school was a run-down madhouse in Crown Heights. The building was falling apart, the staff had not been paid for weeks, some teachers had quit, others were in the office screaming that they were going to go to court. A rabbi in a synagogue a few doors away had died and a crowd of mourners was pushing and shoving in the street to get closer to the plain pine box as it was carried on the shoulders of disciples from the temple to a hearse parked at the curb. One of the teachers I met at the yeshiva that day was named Harvey. I told him I really wasn't interested in teaching, I wanted to be an actor. He told me he was an actor and asked if I had gone to the open auditions for the Broadway play *Compulsion*. I said no. He gave me the name and address of the casting agent.

I went to the casting director's office the next day. There were no auditions for *Compulsion*. There were framed posters of playbills all around the office, plays from the twenties to the present, plays featuring the Lunts, Noël Coward, Jacob Ben-Ami. A secretary told me I could leave a picture and résumé. I had no idea what she meant. She smiled and slowly shook her head. "This," she said, reaching into a folder on her desk and pulling out a glossy head-shot with a résumé pinned to the back, "you'll need one of these. Just drop one off sometime." I thanked her and left.

On my way out of the building, I ran into an old Cherry Lawn classmate, Bob Weiner, who had never really been a friend but now just happened to be a theatrical producer. He was literally right in my face when the elevator doors opened.

"Siff!"

"Weiner!"

"Holy shit!"

We decided to have lunch. I told him I was starting out as an actor. He told me about some of the shows he had done in Chicago, some things he was hoping to do in New York. We smiled in an air bubble of surprise. I told him about the experience I had just had, wanting to audition for *Compulsion*. He told me I needed an agent as well as a good photographer. After lunch, he invited me to his office, where he gave me the name of a photographer and then placed two calls to two different agents, who both agreed to see me that afternoon.

The first agent was a tall, balding man named Abe Newborn. He looked as if he had a bottled tan. Staring at me as I sat nervously across the way from him, he explained that I was a good commercial type but that he knew nothing about me and would have to see photographs before he began to send me out.

The second agent, Stark Hesseltine, had ears that stuck out like the stop signs on a school bus. He also had a tan, but this one was in peeling layers, which made him look as if he had a second face under the first. Stark was the hottest young agent at MCA, in those days the hottest of talent agencies on both coasts. In New York, MCA occupied an entire building on Madison Avenue. The architrave over its front doors framed a stone globe shrunk to the size of a bowling ball. The office interiors were done in English style, oak, leather, brass, and gilt-framed prints of eighteenth- and nineteenth-century scenes of the hunt.

Stark sent me out—immediately. He, too, said he wanted to see pictures, and he wanted me to audition a scene for him and Maynard Morris, MCA's senior agent. But he also set up an audition for me for an upcoming off-Broadway production of Lorca's *Blood Wedding*, the senior play I had skipped out on for baseball practice at Cherry Lawn.

I auditioned for both the Bridegroom and the Lover. I was kept in the upstairs lobby of the theater—the Actors' Playhouse in the Village—with a group of other actors until my name was called and I was led down the stairs into a small, darkened auditorium whose seats were raked up from a bare and dismally lit floor. I held a soft-covered script in one hand, gestured with the other. It was all I could do to keep my hand steady enough to be able to read the words on the page. I wanted to keep eye contact with the stage manager as I read, but the best I could do was a furtive glance or two.

Very nice, thank you, said the director, a woman named Patricia Newhall. She called Stark that afternoon, offering me the part of the Bridegroom. This was nine days after my parents met me at the train station when I returned from Iowa. For the next five years, I was a professional actor. I worked on Broadway and off-Broadway, in New York and California.

What did my mother think of all this? Some time following *Blood Wedding* (which was well received and ran for about a
year), I had gotten my own apartment; I was in the downtown swim of things. My mother called me one day and
asked if we could have lunch together. I agreed, but it seemed
like a strange request, since I saw my parents often, sponging
meals from them, borrowing my father's car whenever I
could. I asked her if something was wrong. She said no, she
just felt like having lunch. We met at a cafeteria near Columbia, not too far from my apartment on the Upper West Side.

I made a journal entry at the time:

> Jan. 23, 1959. My mother's all dolled up.
> What's she trying to prove? Why the hairdo,
> why the silk dress? Why is she making such
> an effort to look like Claudette Colbert? She
> seems more relaxed and at ease than I've seen
> her for years. Zero hostility between us for
> the first time in a long time. I ask her again if
> there isn't a special reason she wants to get
> together. No, she says, no special reason.
> Then she says, she once wanted to be an
> actress herself. I told her I knew she used to
> go down and watch Eva Le Gallienne. Not
> that, she said, she once really wanted to be an
> actress. Really? I asked her if she had actually
> ever acted? Oh, she said, she never had the
> nerve to walk into a producer's office. That
> was it, nothing more. My mother came all the
> way downtown to tell me that a long time
> ago she hadn't been able to walk into a pro-
> ducer's office. She is the strangest woman on
> the planet.

I believe now, forty years later, my mother was living in a haunted house. She was in all likelihood trying to convince herself she was the reason I had become an actor, not Van Heflin. She was summoning an answer for the midnight silences between herself and my father, for the eerie coincidence that her son, knowing nothing, turned out to be his birth father's son.

How to account for that kind of coincidence? Does blood actually determine one's trade as it does tendencies toward diseases and noses? The literature on genetics demonstrates a clear connection between biology and genetics, but the link between behavior and the genes, especially when biologically connected subjects have had little or no contact with each other, is far more tenuous. There are tantalizing anecdotal accounts of identical twins and triplets separated at birth or in early childhood, for example, who meet years later and discover that their temperaments, even their tastes in clothing and choices of occupation are remarkably similar. But there are no clear studies that prove anything in a genetic sense. Edward O. Wilson, in his book *Consilience: The Unity of Knowledge*, tries to reconcile the claims of behaviorists and geneticists. "People do not merely select roles suited to their native talents and personalities," he says. "Their parents, who possess similar inborn traits, are also likely to create a family atmosphere nurturing development in the same direction. The genes, in other words, help to create a particular environment in which they will find greater expression than would otherwise occur."

Well, I had the genes—and the home. But how to account for the links in the strange chain that led me to the stage? If I hadn't had a cold in those first days home, I might

In my early days as an actor, 1958

never have seen that yeshiva ad for a teacher; if I hadn't answered it, I might never have met Harvey the actor . . . and if I hadn't met Harvey the actor, I might never have had the chance to follow in my birth father's footsteps.

2.

Lee, Docky, Harriet, Morty, my mother, and my father have all come to see *The Rose Tattoo*, starring Viveca Lindfors. Viveca for years has been billed as the next Ingrid Bergman but it hasn't worked out that way. She is playing the part of Rose, the mother, in this production (played in the film by the incomparable Anna Magnani). I am playing the part of Jack Hunter, the sailor enchanted by her daughter ("What are you hunting, Jack?"). Lindfors loves the challenge of the stage but she still tries to keep up in film, putting up with the pressure to be the next Bergman. It is late 1959, and recently she has completed the film *Tempest,* one of those low-budget Paramount spectacles produced by Dino De Laurentiis with a cast of stars on the decline, including Van Heflin, who plays the part of Pugachev, the self-proclaimed Czar Peter III, leader of a Cossack revolt against Catherine the Great (played by Viveca).

Viveca has talked freely to the media and to fellow members of the cast about making bad movies as a way of allowing herself to act on the stage. My family is charmed by Lindfors. They compliment her backstage after our opening-night performance in Fort Lee, New Jersey. My mother shakes her hand, quietly says how much she enjoyed her performance. My father marvels at her Italian accent. Morty goes on for a while about Tennessee Williams and Docky asks her if she has ever played his favorite, Shaw. Viveca smiles, whispers something I cannot pick up; then Docky booms, "And you should be sure to read his prefaces." Before they all leave, she tells my mother to use all her influence to keep me on the stage, because the moviemakers will be sure to try to kidnap me. Both women stand there beaming at me, to the point where I begin to blush.

After the run of *The Rose Tattoo,* Viveca calls my agent, Stark, to let him know that she wants me to play opposite her in an off-Broadway production of *The Trojan Women.* I see her at her East Side brownstone and we talk about the play and her plans for it. She would like to do it downtown, maybe at a

place like the Orpheum Theater on Second Avenue, but after
a while, it becomes clear that there may not be the money to
do the play at all. Some time later, Stark calls and tells me the
plans for the play have fallen through.

Soon afterward, toward the end of 1960, I decide to go to
California. My mother is disturbed by this. Why California?
she wants to know. I have no good answer. It's winter, I'm not
in a play at the moment, it's a good time to go. Stark keeps
talking about the movie department at MCA in California
wanting to work with me. And besides, I say, Hilda and Lou
have moved back out there, they've even invited me to live
with them. I can't begin to figure why my mother should care
one way or the other about my going or staying.

The same djinn that accompanied me from Iowa to New
York seems to have gone along for the ride to California. A
continent of winter and then, one morning, out the sleeper
window, a vista of crumpled hills in pastel shades of blue and
green. People are in shirtsleeves and sandals in the old
Spanish-style railroad station in Los Angeles, there is a certain perfumed odor in the air—summer in January. The day
after I settle in with Hilda and Lou, he lends me his car so I
can go and meet my new agents.

The MCA building in Beverly Hills seductively suggests
Tara, the White House, or some other familiar dream man-
sion. Inside, the rooms and offices look exactly like those in
New York.

A plump, immaculately dressed woman with a California
tan ushers me down a corridor to her office, says she is glad to
meet me, Stark and Maynard have told her a lot about me.
After briefly making eye contact, she picks up the phone,
swivels around in her chair so she is facing the window,

which looks out on neatly razored rows of hedges. She makes a call to someone named Pat and chats amicably for a couple of minutes, swiveling around to write something down on a pad before she hangs up. When she looks across at me again, she tears off what she has written on her pad. She has made an appointment for me at Universal Studios.

Lou says I can have the car for the day, and he makes sure I understand how to get to the studio. An hour or so later, I turn up at Revue-Universal and go to an office in a squat, nondescript building. The person who eventually comes out to meet me in the waiting area is a tall, thin, middle-aged man in shirtsleeves. He is wearing a baggy white shirt and a conservative-looking tie. There is something both wasted and avid in his manner, as though he is an accountant at tax time or the business manager of a nursing home.

His office is a room whose predominant color is battleship gray, illuminated by overhead tubes of fluorescent light. There are framed pictures of well-known actors and actresses on the walls, the only show-biz touch in the room.

What have I done, who have I worked with, is there any film on me? The conversation is cut and dried. I have already written it off; I know by now when someone isn't interested in me. Then he says, You're another Tony George. I have no idea what he means, and so I simply smile. He picks up the phone and asks the person on the other end to come downstairs for a minute. A much younger man, also jacketless, wearing a business shirt and tie, turns up. He opens the door, steps into the room. No introductions are made.

"Howard," says Pat, "who . . . is . . . he?" Pat nods in my direction.

The other one shrugs.

"C'mon, who is he?" Silence. Pat begins to lead him, he's restless, energized. What he's asking for is obvious.

"He's another . . . another"—he starts to snap his fingers—"c'mon, Howard, another . . ." *Snap! Snap!*

The other one has his shoulders hunched with a rictus of embarrassment stretched across his teeth.

". . . another *Tony George!*" Pat finally says. The other one's face suddenly melts. He taps himself lightly on the forehead.

"Right! *Righhht!* Of course!"

This person leaves, and then, a minute or so later, Pat gets up from behind his desk, says it has been nice to meet me, and wishes me luck in California. We shake hands.

When I get back, Lou tells me to call my agent at MCA. I do so, and she excitedly informs me that Universal has offered a seven-year term contract. "But they don't know anything about me," I say. There is a laugh on the other end of the phone. "Oh, yes, they do! You're another Tony George!"

I am puzzled and embarrassed. I can barely bring myself to ask the agent the question uppermost in my mind.

"Would you tell me, please: *who* is Tony George?"

The agent laughs. "Very funny."

"Aha," I say, unwilling to pursue this. I've been in California for just three days.

Tony George is the lead actor on a popular television series of the day, *Checkmate.* I am introduced to him one day several weeks later in the studio commissary. He is considerably shorter than I am, has dark, almost Sicilian features, a mat of short wiry black hair, thick closely stitched eyebrows. He is an uncomfortably intense person. I try to be winning and informal. I tell him the funny story about how I came to be a contract player for Revue-Universal.

"I don't think that's very funny," he says, and walks away.

I was lonely in Hollywood. Aside from Hilda and Lou, I didn't know anyone for months. I used to go to Ralph's Supermarket on Doheny Drive late at night hoping to pick up women. One night, I ran into a woman who had had a small part in *Blood Wedding*. We came back to my place. One time only. She was drunk and overweight and I was ashamed of myself.

When I spoke with my parents on the phone, our conversations were almost always about New York, my brother and sister, how Grandma was doing. My parents were both touched by the gifts I had sent them—a chamois briefcase for my father, a pearl pendant for my mother—thanks to my munificent studio salary of $350 a week. They asked little about what I was doing and I volunteered little beyond making typical jokes about Hollywood: beneath the phony tinsel is the real tinsel.

I really didn't know why I was in Hollywood. In reality, I wasn't working much for my money. I did a couple of screen tests that didn't pan out. I was called in from time to time to do office auditions with a Miss Bolivia or Miss Peru who was unable to speak English, barely able to read lines from a script. I did small parts on television shows: a tennis-playing cad in *Alfred Hitchcock Presents;* an innocent college kid mowed down with his sweetheart in a Cicero speakeasy by the mob on *The Untouchables;* I was in a few Westerns, *Rawhide* and *Wagon Train.* It could never have dawned on me that I was out there looking for my father.

Making one of these Westerns, I become friendly with Brandon de Wilde. As a child actor he was Van Heflin's son in the movie *Shane.* His face was haunting in that movie, round as an angel's, cornsilk hair in a bowlcut on his head, eyes like a deer's.

When we're not in a scene, we take our mounts and ride across Universal's back lot, up and down hills, near the freeway, then down trails that lead into isolated ghost towns built entirely of false fronts. We sit on the front porch of a saloon, on the weatherbeaten planks of the steps, on nail barrels in the shade, with our horses tied to hitching posts. Brandon is no longer a child actor. His face is lean and scruffy. I ask him about *Shane*. No big deal, he says, he literally lived in the theater as a kid because he grew up in a show-business family—mother and father worked backstage all their lives— so it was natural to become an actor, he says, that was what he knew.

Since then his career has been in decline. Like a lot of child stars, he has not made the transition to adult roles well. He has a somewhat fatalistic air about this. He loves sports cars, racing cars. He has one parked in the lot, a thing that looks like a dune buggy but is really a souped-up racer with wheels widely separated on spider axles so the car can corner at high speeds. One day he gets me to ride with him. I'm strapped into the passenger seat like a crash dummy and he takes the car out to the back lot. We ride some of the same dusty stretches we've been over on horseback. He corners a hairpin curve going at least fifty or sixty miles an hour, then, in an open space, guns the engine, hits the brakes, turns the wheel, sends the car into a screeching 360 so that when we come to a stop and the huge dust cloud engulfing us clears we're still pointed in the same direction. He's excited and happy. He tells me if he can't make it as an actor he'll race cars for a living.

I remembered that day on the back lot when I read about the car crash he died in a few years later.

Another time, we walk over to the set of *Judgment at Nuremberg*, which is being filmed at Universal. Brandon knows a lot of the people—Stanley Kramer, Montgomery Clift, Spencer Tracy. On the day we're there, the big scene to be shot is a summation from the bench by the chief judge, played by Tracy. There is a lot of standing around and talking first. Apparently the speech has been changed by the writers and a brand-new one has just been handed to Tracy, who tells Kramer that he'll shoot it but he'll need a few minutes first. He is left to himself sitting on the high bench. He has his glasses on, head bowed, his expression stony and absorbed. Finally, he looks up and says he's ready. Kramer asks him if he wants to try a dry run. He says no. The other actors take their place, the room is quieted, someone materializes from the darkness near the camera with a scene board, calls out a take number, clacks down the arm of the board, then jumps out of the way while someone else shouts "Rolling!" and Tracy, with the barest in-breath, takes off his glasses, looks up from his high perch on the bench, and peers directly into the camera lens pointed at him from the well of the courtroom.

His words come slowly at first, then with quickened pace. His voice is gravelly, full of authority, clarity, and great passion. It is impossible to believe that what he says was written by someone else and memorized only minutes before. The words, the cadences of the sentences, the ideas, the great sweep of eloquence all seem to be his own, coming from some deep cavern of conviction in his body. Every word, every nuance of meaning seems to carry the weight of the world's collective moral condemnation of the Nazis and their monstrous crimes. Tracy is so utterly convincing that when he finishes there is a kind of breathless silence in the room, as though all available oxygen in the hangar of the soundstage has been sucked up. Then the set erupts. Everyone—actors, grips, lighting people, spectators—breaks into applause. No one is prepared for what follows.

Kramer, his face a bloodless mask, walks across the courtroom floor to the bench where Tracy is sitting and tells him, loud enough for everyone to hear, that the speech will have to be done over again because there was no film in the camera. Tracy seems less affected by this than anyone else. He merely nods and shifts slightly on the bench. Then, when the room is again quieted, and the call for cameras rolling is given, he delivers the speech once more—and if anything, does it with even greater passion and weight of authority, so that when it is over there is not only cheering but screaming. Kramer almost sprints across the room to tell Tracy how brilliant he has been.

A day or so later, at lunchtime, when we break from the Western we are shooting, I walk with Brandon over to the Universal commissary for lunch. The place is crowded with a carnival collection of actors from thirty different soundstages, costumes from ten centuries alongside the plain suits of all the lawyers, agents, and accountants. Brandon spots some people he knows and says he'll be back. I get on line with my tray. When he returns, he asks me if I want to have lunch with Tracy and his friend Van Heflin. He points to a table with several people. I can recognize Tracy. I cannot see Heflin. I think I'll pass, I say. I know Brandon is merely being polite because we had walked over to the commissary together.

In the end, Hollywood was not for me. I lasted about a year, going nowhere, and begged out of my contract before I was fired. I came to California unsure what I was looking for, and once it was clear I was not going to find it, I left and headed back to New York.

SEVEN

When I got back to New York, I moved in with my parents until I began working again. Things had changed in the time I had been away—almost a year. In that time, my grandmother had died and my brother and sister had moved out of the house.

I was told that in my grandmother's final hours she refused blood transfusions—a decision that angered one of her doctors to the point of his asking her if she wanted to die so she could leave money to her daughters. My mother, I was told, fell apart. She got on the phone to the hospital administrator and demanded that the doctor be taken off the case. The administrator apologized. "I don't care," my mother was supposed to have said. "My mother can only die once. I just want someone to be nice to her tonight, that's all."

I can only imagine what the loss of her mother meant to her. In so many ways, my grandmother was a link between worlds for my mother, connecting her to all the choices she had made in her own life—like whom she married—but equally connecting her, through loyalty, devotion, and guilt, to the immigrant world of her parents. The consequences were inevitable. She drew great strength from her mother, learning from her many practical ways of running a household: what to look for in shopping, how to maintain a kitchen and a family budget, how to deal with the competing interests of various family members. She learned even more from her about the value of stoicism and the ability to convert hardship into something else. But she also surrendered a piece of her own life in the process.

After my grandmother's death, my mother quit the job she had had for a while with the city government, saying she just wasn't up to working anymore. She was in the midst of a watershed year. Not only had she lost her mother, but in that same period her children dropped away from her as well. I moved to California; my brother moved out of the house to begin his first year of law school; my sister, Judy—the "baby"—began her freshman year at the University of Michigan. For the first time in her married life, my mother found herself living alone with my father.

I thought at first my mother was sorry to see me back in New York. She kept asking me why I'd left California, and no answer I gave seemed to satisfy her. She always had this maddening way of conveying the sense that, of course, whatever anyone was saying was hiding something deeper. I insisted that California simply wasn't for me, that I wanted to be in theater, not film. She didn't buy it.

"What's wrong?" she asked one day when she saw me in the kitchen, by myself, eating breakfast. She had a somber look on her face. "Nothing," I insisted. She stared at me. Then I started to laugh at her and she threw up her hands and walked away.

Because my mother was just unable to relent, I wanted to find my own place as soon as possible. Yet I felt comfortable—comforted—living with my parents. I slept as late as I wanted, I was fed every day, and I borrowed my father's car whenever I wanted to go into the city—which was most days and certainly every night. I scarcely took note of my mother in this new part of *her* life.

Whenever I was around my parents and their friends, I performed for them. I told them Hollywood stories. There was one about the Universal Studios Executive of the Year (I'm not sure if this was true or I made it up), about a guy who wangled a deal with the state of California to bulldoze part of a mountain range on the back lot of the studio and then turned around and sold the bulldozed dirt back to the state for a huge profit. I embellished stories about stars in the commissary—overhearing Ronald Reagan, then the host for *GE Theater*, who was seated at the next table one day at lunch, saying the way to get Russian missiles out of Cuba was to reduce Cuba to ash and rubble. I told them my Tony George story; I told them how I rode around with crazy Brandon de Wilde.

I moved out of my parents' house as soon as I had enough money. I did parts in a couple of soap operas, and then I was cast in a play—Arthur Kopit's *Oh Dad, Poor Dad, Mama's Hung*

You in the Closet and I'm Feelin' So Sad. I had a small role—one of four bellboys—and was supposed to understudy one of the leads, Austin Pendleton. I found a tiny apartment—a closet-sized room in the West Village that cost sixty dollars a month. I thought I was as ready as I needed to be to continue my life as a struggling young actor. But I wasn't.

I made fun of the shows I was in, the small soap-opera parts I did, even *Oh Dad*, one of the prestigious plays of the season. I hated my part, thought the play was overrated; I told myself Jerome Robbins couldn't direct, Arthur Kopit couldn't write, Austin Pendleton couldn't act (though, in reality, I was intensely jealous of him; he had once been a gofer at Williamstown when I was there doing a lead in a play).

One day, I came in for an understudy rehearsal and was told I was no longer going to be Austin's stand-in because I couldn't fit into his costumes, and a new set would have had to be made for me; the producers didn't want to spend money for that. One of the other bellboys was given the job. I still had my part, my few lines and a bit of shtick. Big deal, I told myself, it didn't matter. But it did. Tallulah Bankhead said there was no such thing as small parts, only small actors. Tallulah was never a bellboy in a Kopit play.

I began playing poker backstage with the stagehands. Actors and stagehands belong to different worlds. I joined their world. They played every day at a table in a rear area behind the set where anyone passing by from the dressing rooms could see them. Their games started when they came in and lasted right through the show, interrupted only for scene changes. They played longer games on matinee days. Sometimes they would play for a couple of hours after a show, before locking up for the night.

I was told after a while to cut it out. The stage manager came to me one evening after I nearly missed one of my bell-boy entrances and asked me to stop playing during performances. I left off for a few days—but was soon back at it. I was making good money playing poker. I knew how to play, and as long as the stagehands let me into their game (and as long as I kept winning), there was no way I was going to get out voluntarily.

I knew I was in trouble, however. Every time the stage manager passed by backstage, he saw me, cards in hand. When he saw me there during a performance, he reminded me that he had asked me not to play. I told him that I hadn't missed any entrances and wouldn't. Some time after that, I got a letter from the producers telling me that I was fired. I called my agent. Stark told me things like this happened. They wouldn't have raised an eyebrow if I had had a bigger part, he said.

Exactly, I told myself.

"Not to worry," he insisted, "onward and upward."

Onward and upward to what? I was glad to be out of it. Each day that I turned up at the theater, except for my poker playing, I hated what I was doing—and I hated myself for feeling that way. I didn't feel like an actor at all, I felt like a thief. I looked forward to my poker winnings. My ambition, my passion went into focusing on remembering who had what cards each hand. I got excited when I remembered that a king or a seven of spades had been folded in an early round and the pot was hanging on whether the guy across the table from me had a king or a seven in his hand. Excitement drained from me when it was time to go out onstage and stand there like a mute, watching actors with real parts do their thing.

I don't remember the exact sequence of the next part of my life. I visited an old friend from Williamstown one night (this was during the run of *Oh Dad*), who was a friend of Austin's. She had a roommate, Jenny, whom I fell in love with. In one night. I saw her sitting there and I told myself, She's for me—as though it had been arranged in the stars. Like me, she was an actor on the margins and a little jaded about it. She had been a dancer at Stratford when Robert Ryan and Katharine Hepburn had done *Antony and Cleopatra* together. She was full of stories about them and Spencer Tracy, who had hung around that whole summer with Hepburn. Jenny did a merciless imitation of Ryan trying to mouth the words, in Brooklynese, "Egypt, I'm dying. I'm dying, Egypt."

Jenny was beautiful and smart—she looked like Shakespearean royalty herself, a younger Cleopatra, Latin-style. She had been born in Mexico and raised there by American parents. Her mind swam with images of "Los Niños Héroes," the boy who wrapped himself in the Mexican flag and threw himself off the parapets of the Chapultepec Castle and the seven other boys who were gunned down by *yanqui* invaders. Her memories were about paradisiacal swimming holes and banana trees, mysterious villages, sorcerers, and muralists. Diego Rivera and Frida Kahlo were next-door neighbors. She said she had learned how to talk to tarantulas. She was a voracious reader and a lively conversationalist with strong opinions—except when it came to herself as an actress. She laughed at her portfolio, which was filled with corny commercial shots that had been done before she came to the States. There was one in which she held up a jar of Hellman's mayonnaise, a look of open-eyed surprise on her face, as though someone had just goosed her; in another, she smiled under a glittering tiara that made her look more like one of the last of the Romanovs.

I don't remember if I was still in the play or out when I introduced her to my parents. From the first moment, it was oil and water. We sat through a quiet meal. They didn't say much to each other. My parents' questions to her were strained and too polite: Where in Mexico had she grown up? How long had she been in the United States? Did she enjoy living in New York? This was unlike my parents, especially my mother, who usually fussed over girlfriends I brought home.

My mother, of course, sensed that Jenny was different from the others. Perhaps she was jealous—but there was really more to it than that. Jenny, for me, represented a lure to leave the theater—and my mother picked up on that.

Soon after I was fired from *Oh Dad*, I told myself I wanted to take a responsible, nine-to-five job. My mother curled her lip at the idea. "Why?" she asked. "Because I want to," I said. She then seemed to ambush me with little asides questioning my desire to be an actor. One time, she asked why I didn't go to see more plays. "Money," I said. "*Bull*," she whispered in reply. Another time, when I stayed over at my parents' house one weekend, she saw me dive for the sports section of the Sunday *Times* at breakfast. "You know, it's really curious that you don't seem interested in the arts section," she said. I looked up at her. "What's that supposed to mean?" "Nothing," she answered. "I just think it's strange that someone who's an actor wouldn't be interested in the section of the paper that was about the theater."

My mother's instinct was painfully correct. I was disengaging from the theater and didn't even know it. From the minute I got up in the morning, I was preoccupied with how little money I had. I counted the days until my next unemployment check. My habits and routines changed. I avoided my actor friends, stayed away from haunts like the Actors' Equity lounge or Downey's, the bar/restaurant on Eighth Avenue. I could not bring myself to call my agent, who didn't want to hear from me anyway. The next step appeared to me out of my boredom as out of a mist: I could find a job through my mother's connections with the city government.

She reacted coolly. Why would I want a job with the city? she asked. I was an *actor*. Actors needed to eat, I reminded her. But you're hardly in danger of starving my dear, she said, with that knowing look. I didn't answer.

Then she became earnest. "David, your father and I will give you whatever you need to tide you over. You know that."

"I know," I said, "but I need a job."

My mother, as I suspected she would, helped me find one. She called a few days later and told me she had spoken to the city rent commissioner, Hortense Gabel, an old friend of hers, who invited me to call her. Gabel sounded as if she knew me. Her manner on the phone was not only friendly but almost intimate. She asked me to come in and see her whenever it was convenient.

When I turned up at her office, a room with tastefully arranged photographs of her with well-known political and other public figures, she closed the door, hugged me, stepped back, and looked me over.

"My, my, my!" she said, shaking her head with her hands clasped in front of her. She motioned for me to take a seat.

After the preliminaries, she told me that she would arrange for an entry-level job for me with one of the district offices and that I could begin as soon as I wanted. I thanked her, and then she apologized for not having come to any of the plays I had been in. She seemed to know all about me. She had actually gotten tickets to see *Blood Wedding* when I was in that, she explained, but had had to cancel at the last minute.

"Your mother is so proud of you," she said.

She was a large, friendly woman with thick-as-Coke-bottle glasses that magnified her eyes, one of which was unmoving. When I asked her how long she had known my mother, she laughed and said always. She was a friend of Harriet's, she explained, and told me how she used to spend time at my grandparents' home when she was young, her voice becoming almost dreamy. Your mother was so beautiful then, she said; how I liked spending time at the house, just because your mother was there. She kept smiling and staring at me as she talked. Finally, at one point, she laughed and said, almost to herself, "Oh, God, I just don't *believe* this!" "What?" I murmured. "You look just the way you did when you were two!" she said. I nodded uncomfortably. She shook her head and laughed. "David! David! David!"

The job I took told me, as nothing else could, how adrift I really was. I have absolutely no memory of what I did. I had a desk in a room full of desks. On one side of the room, there was a row of desks for senior staff. The unit head of the section had his desk separated from the others by five or ten feet of bare floor space—I guess for appearances' sake. But this unit head was just another lackey himself. Often, he would follow the deputy assistant director (who had a private office) up and down the corridors, striding just a foot or two behind him wherever he went. An elderly woman who sat at the desk in front of mine, and to whom I had never talked, turned to me one day after the unit head had just passed by on the heels of the deputy assistant director. "If Margolis stops short, they'll have to dig Shub out of his asshole," she said.

I couldn't have lasted in my job more than a few months. It was all the incentive I needed to start thinking seriously about what I wanted to do with my life. I eventually decided to go back to graduate school. I'm not sure just how this evolved, but it was out of the matrix of one too many days at the Rent Commission. Graduate school would be preferable, for sure. It seemed like the ideal compromise: a responsible job, the ability to look after myself—with lots of time off.

I told Jenny first—and she didn't seem impressed: "If that's what you have to do, I guess you have to do it." I asked her why she seemed turned off, and she said she thought I was an actor, not a professor.

When I told my mother, she was far more upset and much less direct. Was I sure I knew what I was doing? Had I become discouraged? she wanted to know, because, if so, there was really no reason to be. Her face was drawn and very earnest, a sure indication that she wasn't about to tell me what was on her mind. I tried to explain to her that I felt it was time for me to make a regular life for myself. But it was as though I had said nothing. Had I really thought out what it meant to turn my back on what I obviously loved? she asked. I was doing so well, I had a career and a future, didn't I know that? Was my agent wrong about me, were all the reviewers who had liked me so much wrong? I smiled but couldn't answer her. She was coming on too strong. What was she up to anyway? She looked at me the way she had when I was a child, conveying to me the conspiratorial sense that we were in something together, that what I felt she knew perfectly, that what she felt I, too, young as I was, knew just as well.

I tried to shrug her off. "Ma, it's okay," I said.

She slowly shook her head, but she didn't turn away in exasperation—as I hoped she might. Instead, she continued to stare at me. I could see in the set look on her face that she was actually angry. "Your secret, David, whether you know it or not, is that you are a very conventional person."

I'm not sure if I said anything, if I held up a hand or walked away. I felt hurt—because she called me conventional, but even more over the disapproval I heard in her voice.

There was at least one more flare-up, which I remember even less distinctly. I was at my parents' apartment for dinner one night. We must have gotten into a quarrel or a contentious discussion about something. I remember I was sitting on the floor of their bedroom with my back up against a closet door; my mother was sitting on her bed, smoking; my father was at his desk, twisted around in his chair to face me. I don't know what they said that provoked me, but I told them—very dramatically—"You don't know who I am!" I remember the stricken look on my mother's face.

"What are you talking about?" she said—just as dramatically.

In that same time period, I applied to and was accepted at UCLA. I chose UCLA because I really had no choice. I knew I could get in, and that I could wangle a state residency for myself (which would mean I would have to pay almost nothing). I also knew it would help me get away from my parents, something I then felt I needed to do.

What I counted on, of course, was that Jenny would

come with me to California. I did not anticipate that she wouldn't. I knew she wasn't thrilled about my decision, but I thought she would eventually go along. When my acceptance from UCLA for the spring semester came through, I asked her, and she declined. We had been living with each other for several months, and though there were serious differences between us, we got along, enjoyed each other's company. Jenny said she wanted to go back to Mexico for a while and wouldn't decide anything until after Christmas. The day she packed up and left, I drove her to the airport. All the way to Idlewild, we didn't speak.

"Ta ta," Jenny said, without kissing me at the gate to the plane. I watched her disappear in the stream of boarding passengers and then walked back to the parking lot, feeling empty and confused. This was *not* in my plans.

In the weeks that followed, I was unsure that I would even go to California. I simply had not thought through the idea of going back there alone—and not even as an actor. A few weeks after she left, I phoned Jenny in Mexico. I remember the day, in early November. I can still see the pattern of weak-tea sunlight outside my ground-floor barred window on Charles Street, the empty late-morning street, the rattling sound of a trash collection a few doors away. Jenny's voice came over the receiver sounding as if she were speaking from another planet. I couldn't tell if she was glad to hear from me, nervous, or surprised. She seemed cheerful in the way she always was when she was deflecting what she felt. She was just on her way out the door, she explained, to work at a Swedish massage parlor, training to get a license as a masseuse. My spirits plummeted. That meant she had already committed herself to staying in Mexico. I asked her how she was. Fine, she said. I told her I missed her. She asked about the cat. (We shared a cat that had jumped in through the bars of the window one night, chased by a streetful of toms who all wound up in the middle of our bed. We woke up, startled nearly to death, and turned the lights on—but then we laughed, chased out the toms, and named our rescued cat Doxie. It was the night William Faulkner died, I noted with great solemnity, and I remember that after we fed Doxie I sat her before us on the bed and intoned the Nobel Prize address to her.)

"She misses you, too," I told Jenny. Then, in the silence that followed, I asked her if she would marry me—and to my amazement she said, very casually, "Sure, why not."

I think my mother had not really believed I was going to leave New York. After Jenny had gone back to Mexico, I told her that my plans weren't as certain as I thought, that I needed a little more time to think. My mother told me she knew I was going through a difficult period and I should take whatever time I needed to figure out what I really wanted. She hoped I understood that anything I decided would be fine, she said. But then I went to my parents' house to tell them that Jenny and I were going to get married. I got there before dinner, before my father had come home from the office. My mother seemed glad to see me, was in good spirits. She was working on a drink, maybe a second. She asked me if I wanted one and didn't wait for an answer, just fixed me a vodka and Clamato juice and invited me to keep her company in the kitchen.

She was banging around the stove, I remember, checking on something in the oven.

"Shit," she said with a smile, "I don't know how long I'm supposed to keep it in." She edged out a roasting pan, sliced into a blackened chunk of meat, saw that it was bloody inside, then pushed the pan back in.

"Ma," I said, when she straightened up, "Jenny and I are getting married." For a second or two she looked as though she hadn't heard. Then she seemed to release a breath, tilting her head to one side, looking at me as though she was trying to figure something out.

"Who's Jenny?" she asked.

At no point then or afterward did she or my father take any interest in the details of the upcoming wedding. Perhaps I had conveyed the impression that it was going to be a private civil ceremony. I'm sure I pointed out to them that it wasn't going to be a church wedding, that a local judge in Cuernavaca, where Jenny's parents lived, would marry us. Whatever I said, when the invitations came, my mother and father decided not to go. I don't remember what excuse they gave, because I didn't really feel hurt. At the time, their decision to stay home seemed natural. In some sense, I was glad that they would not be coming, that I would not have to deal with them, isolated among strangers. I was starting my own life. I certainly didn't question my parents' love for me or have any suspicion that there might have been a division between them over whether or not to attend. I was their firstborn son. Though I don't believe that could have been a source of contention between them, it's possible, I realize, that my father, weary of the role he had played all those years, might have wanted to save money by staying home, and that my mother, in the throes of her own corrosive mood, might have consented to stay put. Or perhaps it was the other way around. Maybe my father wanted to go, but backed off because my mother didn't. Perhaps he observed a recognizably implaca-

Jenny and me on our wedding day,
December 29, 1962

ble and inexplicable darkness that had swept over her and that he had learned long ago to leave alone.

But the simplest of all explanations simply did not register: namely, that my mother did not like my choice of a wife. My mother made a show of her liberal and accepting attitude toward almost everything, but she was also extraordinarily clannish. Jenny was Christian, not Jewish. And though my mother never, never would have acknowledged even the smallest rivulet of prejudice within her, Jenny, to her, was an outsider who did not speak her language or share a modicum of her history, someone whose looks mirrored back not her own weighted, questioning, and vulnerable confusion but an almost glacial lightness of being, seemingly able to deflect with a flash of cool green eyes the fires of any passion. A *goy*. Deep in my mother's psyche, there was her own identity in an exiled family that had survived only by its togetherness in a hostile and unforgiving world, an identity that would not accord to a stranger any of the rights of inclusion.

However, I believe there was possibly another, even deeper reason for my mother's cave-mindedness. In ways that I simply was unable to recognize then, she regarded my leaving the theater as the abandoning of a dream—hers even more than mine—a dream we had shared together from the moment of my birth.

Nineteen sixty-two was an extraordinary year in her life, a year of tremendous loss. It began with the death of her mother, it continued with the departure of her two youngest children, and was completed by my change of career and marriage. My mother, in her cave, was looking at the unraveling of all that she had put together for herself over the years, fashioned out of the certain ruin others had predicted for her, out of a world in which she had not only defied ruin but had been able to triumph over it, exercising a power, competence, and control that enabled her old friend Max Rosenberg to tell me many years later, "Your mother changed the day she got married. She became the matriarch, the spark plug of the family; she ran that home with a will of iron." What impresses me today is that I was never aware of that then. All the while that my mother ran my life, I never for a moment understood that any life choice of mine might be intimately bound to the way she saw herself and all she had accomplished.

EIGHT

1.

My mother and I drifted apart. I had my own life, my own family, my own concerns. For the time I was in California I had almost no contact with her. I was at UCLA, intending to get a graduate degree in English. I drove a cab, Jenny worked in an office. Our day-to-day lives sometimes seemed like cutting-room snippets from old Alfred Hitchcock movies. We lived on a quiet street near Robertson Boulevard and were evicted from our first apartment because pets were not allowed. The landlady, flinty-eyed and stout, with a husband who always seemed to stand two feet behind her, told us that we had a responsibility to the house—same as they did. She and her husband had had to sacrifice having children "for the sake of the house," she explained. When Jenny and I got a place a block away, an old woman stopped us in the street late one afternoon.

"I live across the way from you," she said with a seraphic smile. "I sit at my window and watch you all day long. You're so nice to look at." And there was more:

I picked up a passenger at LAX one evening who had me take him to San Bernardino, seventy-five miles away. When we got to the address he gave me, he jumped out without paying—and ran. I got out and chased him, following him into and out of an apartment hallway to a back lot and a field beyond. I found myself standing in the middle of this field screaming to the starlit night.

A police car stopped me on a street near my home one night. There was no one else around. No one walked on streets in or around Beverly Hills at night. The police pointed a flashlight in my face and demanded ID.

I came home from my job one night, woke Jenny from a deep sleep, and told her I had been in a cab queue at the Beverly Wilshire Hotel for an hour. Was I crazy? Why did I need to wake her and tell her that? she wanted to know. Because I'm going to become a doorman with a whistle so I can go toot, toot, toot to the next cab, I shouted.

That was it. I quit UCLA and we were soon on our way back to New York where, I told myself I would find another graduate school.

For a time, my mother was back in my life—but in a different way. Whatever objections she had to Jenny evaporated once she was a member of the family. With our first child, my mother made herself endlessly available as a babysitter; she organized shopping trips and lunches with Jenny so they could look for things for the baby. Jenny became something of a younger sister. Through my mother's connections with city officials, we were able to move into an apartment in one of the new Mitchell-Lama projects on Columbus Avenue. When my brother, Daniel, got married, he and his wife, Joan, moved in a block away. Lee, nearing ninety, had been set up in an apartment nearby. My mother was behind all of it.

For a time, we got together regularly on Sundays at one house or another. At Christmas, really important for Jenny though never celebrated in my childhood home, my mother put aside her Jewish identity. Years of huddling around a small, not-very-well-polished brass menorah dropped away like a set of baby teeth. She waded in to help us decorate our tree, bake cookies, wrap presents. On Christmas Day, she wore red and white and distributed the presents.

My mother even managed to visit us in Mexico one summer when we had gone off to spend time with Jenny's parents. Jenny was then pregnant with our second child and was in danger of miscarrying in her fifth month. A local doctor in Cuernavaca ordered her to bed and had her take daily injections to slow her contractions. My mother arrived on the scene to help out.

Jenny's mother assumed my mother was there because she thought she, Jenny's mother, was incapable of looking after her own daughter. Adding to the turmoil, Jenny's father was ill at the time. It served no one to have Jenny's mother locked into a belief that an honest offer of help was a surreptitious judgment of her abilities.

When my parents arrived in Cuernavaca, they looked out of place and ill-at-ease. Standing next to them, Jenny's mother looked a foot taller. As a pair, she and my mother seemed a little like Mutt and Jeff. My mother-in-law, sour and ill-tempered, felt obliged to show my parents around. She did—with a vengeance. She had them out of the house early in the morning, on the run to local markets, obscure pyramids, little crafts villages nestled in the summits of mountains. My father, who mainly kept to himself, seemed as indefatigable as a camel. My mother panted along in their wake. When she returned in mid-afternoon, she was spent. It was all she could do to collapse on a terrace chair and wait for Jenny's mother to serve lunch and a trayful of drinks.

My mother trailed around after my daughter, Ellen, who was just barely walking. This was a mistake on her part, because it brought to the surface latent differences with Jenny's mother over childrearing. My mother worried that Ellen might slip, trip, or stumble on the smooth tiles of the terrace or down the rough volcanic stones of the crooked stairway leading to the garden that she was sure harbored a variety of venomous subtropical reptiles. Jenny's mother believed in the learning power of children's falling and then picking themselves up. As my mother wandered around after my daughter, my mother-in-law turned into a latent volcano. "Oh, Eleanor, do come and have a drink! Yoo hoo, Bloody Marys!" she'd call out. My mother would trail after Ellen as though she hadn't heard. One afternoon, when my mother finally did settle down on the patio, she explained how "tippy" Ellen was on her feet. Jenny's mother, looking at her nails, said, "Well, she certainly won't learn to walk with you standing right behind her all the time, will she?"

When it was time for me to go back to school, Jenny still was bedridden. I had to return to New York without her.

Briefly on my own again, I frequently spent time at my parents' apartment on 13th Street, because it was within walking distance of New York University, where I had resumed my studies. I happened to be at my parents' place the day my son was born.

I was taking a shower when my mother told me excitedly that there was a person-to-person call for me from Mexico. It was early evening and since it was early November, it was dark out. I remember walking through the apartment with all the lights blazing, wearing just a towel wrapped around my midsection. When I took the phone, my mother hovered like a cloud over my shoulder. Jenny's mother was calling.

"David," she said, "I have good news and bad news."

"Bad news?"

"What bad news?" my mother said.

"Jenny had a boy. He's fine. But he nearly died coming out."

"Died?"

"He was starting to strangle on his umbilical cord. The doctor saved him. It's lucky he made it."

"Oh my God. But he's okay? Thank God. What about Jenny?"

"Tired but she's all right. The baby's seven pounds, ten ounces. And he has good strong lungs. She named him Ivan."

I repeated everything my mother-in-law told me. My mother was hanging on my shoulder when I got off the phone. All I could think of was that I'd see Jenny and my new son whole and healthy in a couple of weeks. I was almost unaware of my mother but then when I looked at her standing there, I thought something was wrong. She looked vaguely distressed, unsure of her own feet. There was no color in her face. Her eyes were shining, but they were as glassy as marble.

"What's wrong, Ma? The baby's fine, Jenny's okay," I assured her.

"No, no . . . It's just . . . *Ivan?* Whose idea was it to name him Ivan?" she said.

2.

I finished graduate school around the same time my sister Judy got married. What should have been a festive time was really bittersweet, because it marked a further breaking up of our family. With my doctorate nearly in hand, I went to the annual Modern Language Association convention that year and wound up with two job offers—one from the University of Massachusetts, the other from the University of Wisconsin. I chose Wisconsin. My sister, who had transferred during her undergraduate years to an art school in Philadelphia, married someone she knew from Michigan and moved with him back to Detroit, where he had a job teaching English at Wayne State.

Just as my mother had a hard time letting go of me, she also had a hard time letting go of Judy. Judy had been a painter in her undergraduate days—and a promising one. She dropped out of the University of Michigan to spend a year abroad studying at an art school in Paris. My mother (and father) supported her. When she returned to the United States, she went to the Philadelphia Academy of Fine Arts, where my mother took a keen and active interest in her program. My mother's involvement became even more obvious when Judy found herself in a kind of struggle with institutional authorities over the kind of painting she was doing.

One day, during a classroom exercise, Judy had been asked by her instructor to select an abstract shape—a triangle, a circle, a square—and experiment with it in clusters of design. The shape she chose was an ovoid, an egg. She didn't know why at first. She made one study of it, a creamy egg against a creamy background. And then she painted clusters of eggs, as the assignment called for. She was praised for this. But days later, when the next exercise was given, she continued to paint eggs. Her teachers advised her to move on, but she couldn't. She could no more stop painting eggs than Mondrian could stop painting rectangles.

My mother rallied to my sister's side, becoming her champion against the wall of negative opinion she had run into. She was very practical in her support. Not only did she encourage Judy, she made a point of framing all her paintings—and as time passed and Judy's imagination opened, the paintings of egg shapes flowered into wall-sized murals. My mother made sure each of them was hung in one house or another—my parents' home, my brother's, mine, Harriet and Morty's, Lee's.

It was obvious my mother was not happy when Judy got married. At the wedding ceremony—at my parents' apartment in New York—my mother had one too many and clearly was out of sorts. She did not particularly take to her new son-in-law, a thin, shifty-eyed Midwesterner from a prominent family who wrote poetry (which she dismissed as cold) and seemed to her something of a misogynist. She was sure he didn't really care about Judy's painting and didn't love her—and she said so, sitting off in a corner after the ceremony, quietly hanging on to a cigarette and a drink. "You know, two days ago Judy came to me and said she didn't want to marry him and I actually talked her into going through with it," she said miserably.

After Judy got married and moved away, she and her husband became caught up in radical politics. They were married in 1967, as protests against the war in Vietnam were accelerating. Their marriage did not last but their political involvement did. They moved from Detroit to Seattle after a year. Photographs of my brother-in-law disrupting a rally for Hubert Humphrey, then Democratic candidate for president, appeared in the national press one day. Judy came east that winter, just prior to a scheduled meeting of student radicals in Flint, Michigan. Her visit, in a sense, was a kind of farewell to the family my mother had presided over.

We all came together—Jenny, the children, and I from Wisconsin; Harriet and Morty and their children; Lee; my brother and his family; and Judy—at a large country home near Claverack, New York, which my parents and Harriet and Morty had purchased together the year before. In all, there were eighteen of us, and it was the last time our entire family was together—funerals included—at the same time in the same place.

There was a blizzard that weekend. For a full day, a night, and part of the next morning, snow obliterated nearly everything. It was not possible to move out of this refuge for nearly four days, until a county snowplow finally made it through. The joke in the family was that so much shopping had been done by the women of the house before the blizzard that the snowplow could have taken another week before anyone would have gone hungry. But the snowstorm also exacerbated tensions. Within a day or two of forced togetherness, Harriet's family and my mother's had withdrawn to separate parts of the house, coming together only for meals. My mother and Harriet quarreled incessantly over tiny details of service—whether coasters were needed on the marble table near the fireplace, whether or not separate plates for salad were to be used. I can still hear Paul, Harriet's son, heading for a divorce, going on and on about Ernie Kovaks and the Nairobi Trio; and his wife, a thin, nervous woman, explaining to my brother's wife, Joan, who was frozen with rapt puzzlement, why Roger Sessions was such an important American composer. And I can still hear Morty, Harriet, and my father calling out to Judy to turn off the television—which she kept switching on to catch the latest weather report.

The focus throughout was my mother and Judy. My mother's spirits darkened as the time approached for Judy to leave. It was obvious she would not be able to persuade her daughter to stay, though she wanted to. She had no power over her. In just a matter of months, my mother had become a bystander in her daughter's life.

My mother stayed behind in the house when Judy finally left on the fourth day. My father drove her to the train station. My mother kissed her goodbye in the kitchen, at the door to the patio, but then turned away and walked back inside the house. She stood at the living-room window, looking like one of the Trojan women at the fall of Troy, and watched the car drive away, moving across a long, snow-banked access road. Jenny went up to her and asked if she was all right.

"I have the feeling I'll never see her again," she said, in a low, tragic voice.

*My mother with my brother Daniel's oldest
son, Andrew, around the time my sister, Judy,
went underground*

3.

As Judy's commitment to radical politics deepened, so, too,
did the sense that she had deeper allegiances than the one to
her family. My mother had a hard time watching Judy give up
painting. As an old leftist, she also found it hard to accept her
politics. But she couldn't begin to accept that something mattered more to Judy than her family. My mother visited her in
Detroit and on the West Coast, always with the sense that,
no matter what, Judy was Judy. But when she came back from
these visits, my mother's spirits seemed to spiral downward.

The Vietnam War, it has been tiresomely pointed out,

was generational, dividing young people—all those under thirty—from their elders. The time was such that many families split and fell apart along that dividing line. In my parents' case, the division was a little more complicated. Though my mother disagreed with the politics of the New Left, there was enough of the old socialist in her to feel a kind of kinship with "the movement." She believed violence and revolutionary posturing were wrong and counterproductive, but she was deeply opposed to the war and had a sense of ease around people like my sister and me who became activists. At the University of Wisconsin, I was fired in my first year for antiwar activities on campus. My sister became an antidraft organizer in Seattle, hub of Boeing and neighbor to Fort Lewis, a major Stateside departure point for troops on their way to the war.

My father, on the other hand, was slow to oppose the war (though eventually he did) and never felt anything more than contempt for what he believed was the New Left's scorn for democracy. He did not take kindly to the "counterculture," which he believed was anti-intellectual and contemptuous of real culture. Above all, as a lawyer, dedicated to the law, he could not tolerate any movement—left, right, or in between—that he believed would threaten it.

One day, my sister and her husband were arrested and charged with attempting to plant a firebomb at an ROTC facility on the campus of the University of Washington. The bomb hit the news—and my family—but never actually ignited. My sister and brother-in-law were in jail in Seattle. Both of their families raised money to get them out, and eventually they came east for a while before their scheduled trial. They were facing ten to twenty-five years.

It was an especially tense time. My parents realized they

could not carry on a conversation in their own house for fear that listening devices might have been planted. At least, that's what Judy and her husband had cautioned them about.

My mother and father reacted in different ways. Both of them were worried sick for their daughter, but my mother saw herself as an emotional ally and was better able to adjust to the everyday pressures of life under siege; my father, who surely was interested in knowing more about the upcoming court case facing his daughter, retreated further and further into detachment and silence.

The plan was for Judy and her husband, after a week or so in New York, to go to the Midwest and spend some time with her in-laws before heading back to Seattle to stand trial. The day before she left New York, Judy took my mother out of the house. They went to midtown. Perhaps they did some shopping or had lunch somewhere—Judy was never clear about this. But at one point, Judy walked her into Central Park. They strolled along until they came to a formation of rocks on a small hill, out of the way of passersby. Judy steered her to this place, telling her she had something she wanted to talk about.

She then told my mother that when she and her husband left the next day they had no intention of going back to Seattle for the trial. They would never be able to win a court case, Judy said; the deck was completely stacked against them. They would rather take their chances as fugitives. My mother was startled and upset, but understood why Judy and her husband feared standing trial. How would they manage to survive underground—where would she live, what would she do? she asked. Judy assured her that she had friends in lots of different places and that she would be all right wherever she went. My mother was worried about the dangers and difficulties of staying in touch. Judy then told her that it would not be possible for them to have any contact after she and her husband went underground.

My mother was devastated. She had a harder time accepting this than the prospect of seeing her daughter jailed. You can't do that, she told Judy. She couldn't bear the idea of not knowing if her daughter was all right, if she was alive or dead. Surely, Judy had to know her mother would support her and never do anything to jeopardize her. Judy said she did know that but it was too risky and too dangerous to place her and my father in harm's way. Someday, Judy said, they would surely be in touch again, but not for a while. My mother seemed to be in a state of shock when they climbed down from the rocks.

That night, the night before Judy and her husband left, my mother gave her a locket as a keepsake, a family heirloom that my grandmother had once worn. My mother had placed a picture of herself inside it.

My mother had not seen Esther Menaker in twenty years, but she went to see her, Menaker recalled, shortly after Judy went underground. She was distressed, shaky, and seemed to be in the grips of a profound depression. Menaker believed, however, that my mother had not really sought her out for therapy, but only because she needed someone to talk to.

"The overriding sense I had," she told me decades later, "was how isolated and lonely your mother was. I had the feeling I was the only person in the world she could talk to."

4.

Judy stayed in touch with Jenny and me all through her underground years, though we were honor-bound to say nothing to my parents. I saw what effects the lack of contact had on my parents. My father kept whatever he was feeling to himself; my mother was far easier to read. Outwardly, she was much the same except for unpredictable surges of mood. On a whim, she would swoop up her grandchildren and take them off for a weekend somewhere, or she would suddenly plunge into a housebound torpor, eventually shaking off the effects to throw a party, or to bring weekend guests up to the country.

She began doing volunteer work for the Emergency Civil Liberties Committee (ECLU), a left-leaning group that had split off from the ACLU during the McCarthy years. She tried—and failed—to organize a First Amendment study group. She spent time with Edith Tiger, the director of the ECLU. Tiger, like Menaker, believed my mother was broken-hearted over the loss of her daughter and came down to the offices in the Flatiron Building mainly because she needed someone to talk to. Out of these conversations, my mother put together a benefit art sale—that would feature her daughter's paintings—to be held on the lawn of her home in Claverack. It was one more way, perhaps, of holding on.

Judy's paintings and drawings, along with a few donated Calders and Evergoods, were hung from clotheslines or propped against trees. But it rained that weekend, and no pictures were sold. The sky darkened, the wind whipped up, the pictures were cleared away. The few guests who had turned up sat around in the living room. My mother stood at a window watching the rain, as though it were a steel cage clamped down over her life.

Finally, at one point, Judy wanted to see my mother. It had been a couple of years. I had by then been fired from Wisconsin, been hired by Brooklyn College, and had settled within commuting distance, not far from Claverack. Judy got in touch with Jenny and me. We met her in Albany one day and set up a tentative plan to bring my parents there to see her.

I went to Claverack and told my parents, walking with them down to the redwood swings near the pond. My mother cried; I could not tell what my father felt.

Jenny and I drove my parents up to Albany the next afternoon. They were both quiet in the car, but the tension between them was obvious, especially when I made a point of detouring off and then back on to the Taconic Parkway to make sure we weren't being followed.

My mother and Judy threw themselves into each other's arms, but my father stayed in the background, almost as if he weren't there. Occasionally, during the hour or so we were all together, he would reach out and impulsively grab Judy's hand and kiss it. But he never said a word, whereas my mother and Judy were like two long-lost college roommates.

There were one or two more times when the three of them got together, but it was too hard on my father, and eventually my mother wound up seeing Judy by herself. My mother had different views of what seeing her meant. They didn't confide in me but they didn't have to. My mother was happy to see her daughter, that was all. No fear of what anyone could do to her, no fear of the police, the state, the polit-

ical "climate," superseded this primitive and elemental connection of heart.

My father, in all likelihood, could never get over the idea
that his daughter was a fugitive. And there was in his mind a
connection, just as elemental and primitive, with what that
meant. He had all those terrifying memories of Russia and the
civil war: the flight with his father from town to town, from
hiding place to hiding place. And then, of course, there was
the question of the law. My father believed in it as only someone who had experienced life in a lawless society could have.
He would never turn his daughter in, but he could not get
himself to the point where he consciously accepted being a
lawbreaker himself.

My parents' differences in their views were in the end
superficial. Over the years, they had become, like many married couples, two different trees grafted onto a single trunk.
Their differences, however profound, were not so strong as
their dependence on one another. But now the grafting
seemed to be coming apart, as though its single root system
bizarrely fed one part of the tree but not the other.

My father was dying.

One late-spring day in 1975, my family and I went to visit
my parents at their country home. Harriet and Morty weren't
around, nor was my father. My mother was lying on a lounger
behind the house, buried in a crossword puzzle. She got up to
greet us and walked back to the house to fix some lunch.
When I asked her where everyone was, she said Harriet and
Morty had gone to Poughkeepsie and my father was painting. Painting? My father hadn't touched a paintbrush in years.

"He said he wanted to paint, he went out this morning.
Why don't you go get him? He said he would come in for
lunch."

Really curious, I went traipsing across the long field, crossing over a low stone wall into another field. At a rise, I saw him in the distance, seated at an easel. He was wearing a straw hat—it looked like the same one he had had years ago. As I got closer, I could see that he had two different paintbrushes in his teeth as well as the one in his hand. I smiled and waved but he kept painting.

It was a warm day, I remember. The underbrush was all green, the first daffodils and wild irises of the season were out, and there was a strong noontime blare in the underbrush. I was starting to say something as I approached but stopped when I drew abreast of my father's canvas and saw what he was painting. It was a winterscape.

From where he was sitting, he was looking across a field, past clumps of trees in leaf, to a long curved road sweeping away from the house. But in his painting everything was under a mantle of snow. The trees in leaf had become evergreens, dark and tight against the background of snow and ice. There was no attempt at real detail. The field was just a wide swath of white, the curve of the road a white scar on white. The house was not visible, only a corner of a separate outbuilding, white with the dark edges of a door frame so the building could be distinguished in the snow, and then the columns of evergreen trees, stern as sentries. The sky overhead—though it was bright noon—was midnight blue. There were figures of birds against the sky, birds black as crows and with no more definition than inkblots.

I asked him how come he was painting a winter scene in spring. Still daubing the canvas with white paint, brushes in his teeth, he said, mushily but distinctly: "Because I'll never get out here to see this in December." At the time, I thought what he said was funny.

But it was no joke. My father died the following September, three months before the first snow of the season, three months before I found out he was not my father.

5.

One Friday, my mother and father had driven up to Claverack with Harriet and Morty. Some time around eleven, when they were all sitting down to watch the late news on television, my father complained he was having chest pains. After a few minutes, he said he was feeling better. But the chest pains returned. My mother phoned for an ambulance. By coincidence, my year-and-a-half-old youngest child, Maggie, suffering from a series of undiagnosed high fevers, was then in the same hospital where my father was about to be taken.

My father was carried to the ambulance for the ride from Claverack to Hudson, about twelve miles away. My mother rode with him, sitting next to him, holding his hand. Harriet and Morty followed in a car. My father was awake and joking with an attendant who gave him a preliminary EKG on a portable machine. The reading was normal, the attendant told my mother. My father said he had a confession to make: nothing was wrong with him; the only reason he was going to the hospital was to be with his granddaughter. Those were his last words. He suddenly sat up on his gurney and vomited. Some of the vomit splashed on my mother's clothes. The ambulance was still a few minutes away from the hospital, and there was no CPR equipment in the vehicle. The doctors later said that in all likelihood he was dead before his body fell back against the mattress. My mother said she knew he was dead, too. She waited while an attendant tried frantically to revive him.

Harriet and Morty arrived at the hospital a minute or so after the ambulance. They kept my mother company in the corridor outside the room where my father was being worked on. My mother knew that Jenny was spending the night in the hospital with Maggie, so she went over to a nurses' station and asked someone to call upstairs and have her paged. By the time Jenny came down to join my mother a few minutes later, the doctors had come out of the treatment room to tell her what she already knew.

When Jenny called, she woke me out of a deep sleep. Perhaps for that reason, her news somehow did not surprise me. When I heard her voice I knew she was not calling about Maggie. What she said seemed almost like a puzzle piece sliding into place, another square of moonlight on the bedroom floor. She told me my father had died and she and my mother and Harriet and Morty would shortly be driving to our house.

I remember that I got to my feet then and slowly walked through the house. After checking the bedroom where the other children were sleeping, I went downstairs. I walked through the bedroom where Maggie's empty crib was, through the large living room with its heavy carpeting patterned in moonlight, into the kitchen, where the linoleum floor felt cool as glass against my bare feet. I turned around and walked back into the living room. I kept up this pacing, slow as a Chinese morning exercise, as though there were some purpose to it. All at once, I found myself on my knees. It was as though I came to a spot on the floor and found myself able to continue moving only by going downward. On my knees, I touched my head to the floor, once to the north, once to the south, once to the east, once to the west. There were no words, no prayers, no thoughts. Then I got to my feet and resumed my slow pacing.

When Jenny, my mother, and my aunt and uncle arrived, I saw the headlights from their car stabbing across the wide field as they turned in from the parkway. I switched on the kitchen lights and met them at the door. There were no tears, wailing, or clinging to one another. My mother seemed strangely excited.

We sat in the kitchen until the children came downstairs in the morning, and we told them. They did not seem to be caught in the same spell. Ellen, who was ten then, went to her sister's room by herself, sat on a toy chest with her face propped in her hands like Rodin's *Thinker*, then burst into tears when Jenny and I came into the room a short while later. Ivan, two years younger than Ellen, was out by the stream at the back of the house, flinging stones into the water. When we asked him why he was doing that, he said he was angry—at us—for telling him something he didn't want to hear. Eventually we all had breakfast together, sitting around the kitchen table, mostly in silence, as the sun gradually filled the room with light.

The funeral was hastily arranged and took place while Maggie was still in the hospital. Jenny stayed behind with her through the morning hours the day of the service in the city, meeting us later at a small Jewish cemetery outside Pough-keepsie.

The words, prayers, and eulogies were as strange as the custard-colored rooms of the mortuary, the closed, plain coffin with its raised Star of David, and the little country village of headstones, plaques, and mausoleums where he was buried. Throughout, my mother reminded me of my grandmother. She was stoic, almost serene, as she greeted mourners, seemingly more interested in comforting them than in receiving comfort herself. It was really the first time I had been able to notice her. I saw how small she was. My grandmother was a stout woman, solid and powerful-looking. My mother was a wisp of a woman; a breeze could have lifted her off the ground. She was swallowed up by the mourners who surrounded her. My brother and I took her by the elbows at the graveside to support her when the rabbi intoned Kaddish. I remember, vaguely, that I was surprised she let us do that, because she had seemed so much stronger than her grief.

There was no *shiva* for my father. We were not a family of believers. When the burial service was done that Sunday, the mourners—about fifteen or twenty of them—went back to Claverack for a catered lunch and were gone by midafternoon. My mother stayed behind for another day with Harriet and Morty, who postponed their usual Monday trip back to the city. Then, at her insistence, they took her to New York. When she closed the door of her apartment that day, it was the first time in her life she found herself living alone. Her family, the one she had quietly ruled for almost forty years, had been reduced, one member after another, through age, flight, marriage, and now death, to herself. She had become her own family.

She was sixty years old.

NINE

1.

I think my father had known what I was about to discover. The way it happened still makes me wonder. The signs and advance warnings were thick as thunderclouds on the plains. You didn't have to be a wizard or a psychic to notice them.

First, there were dreams, obvious ones. For almost a year before finding out about my adoption, I had dreams that I belonged to another family, had other siblings. There was one in which I came home to a hut in the woods. A figure was sitting in a corner near the fireplace. He had dark hair, strange features; I had never seen him before. I was amazed when I realized he was my brother. I also had dreams right after my father's death. In one, he was walking along a beach in the Caribbean (or someplace that looked like that), nattily dressed, his hair slicked back Valentino-style, and he was on his way to play a game of bridge. He looked happy. He turned, saw me, and motioned for me to follow him, saying that he had something to tell me—but I woke up instead. In another dream, we were driving along the Taconic Parkway on a bright, cloudless day. I switched on the radio. An announcer was giving the weather report: clear skies for the next five days. "No," my father said, "there's a storm coming."

Then there was the matter of astrology. Before he died, my father suddenly got upset about my interest in astrology. In those counterculture years, my father had a hard time tolerating my long hair, the slogan buttons on my vest, the drugs in my pockets. But astrology ranked right at the top of his list of irritants, alongside the wisdom of Chairman Mao. Normally, we avoided any discussion of it—same as with Chairman Mao—but one time we got into a huge, crazy row.

About two weeks before his death, he and my mother came over to babysit one night. I was upstairs getting ready when they arrived. I hadn't bothered to clear my astrology books off the worktable in the living room. I was preparing a chart for my daughter Maggie, whose medical problems had not yet been diagnosed. Suddenly my father's voice grew loud. Something was wrong, I didn't know what. I couldn't imagine him quarreling with Jenny. I finished pulling on my shirt and hurried downstairs. He was standing at my desk with one of my astrology books in his hand. When he saw me he wanted to know what I thought I was doing. I didn't know what he meant—and didn't really want to. He let me know anyway.

"You think you're going to make your daughter better with astrology?"

I could feel the air slowly escaping the room. "I don't think anything," I said quietly.

I don't know what I said or he said after that, but just like that the book in his hand went sailing across the room, hit a wall, and fell to the floor. My mother and Jenny came running. My mother pulled at my father's arm; Jenny pushed me out the door, where the children were standing and watching open-mouthed.

Two weeks later he was dead. But that wasn't the end of it. Days after he died, I was sleeping downstairs on a couch in the living room when I was awakened by a loud sound. I sat upright in bed, not knowing what it was I heard. Then I heard it again, a loud, dry, sizzling sound from a corner of the room, near my desk. I switched on a lamp and got out of bed and walked over to the desk where my astrology books were. There was a cicada against the wall. I could see its dark body and fuzzed legs through its transparent wings. Over and over again—as though it was in a fury—it made its hard, sizzling chirr. I crouched down, staring at it—crazily remembering the scene I had been through with my father. Then I went to the kitchen, got a glass, put the mouth of it over the insect, slipped a three-by-five card underneath, and gently lifted the cicada from the floor. I walked it to the kitchen door and said goodbye as I released it into the night.

Of course, I know now why my father was so worked up: astrology was leading directly to the discovery of my parents' secret.

This is the way it happened:

First, there was the business of my daughter's illness. The

first chart I cast for her said her illness was serious. When we finally took her to see specialists in New York, she was diagnosed as having a third kidney. We were shown an X ray of a milky cloud sitting atop her ruined urinary-tract system like the blighting cocoon of a tent caterpillar. The surgeon said that an extensive operation would be necessary and that there was a chance Maggie might not survive it. We were given a date for the operation—and then I cast another horoscope.

The chart for that day was a disaster. I employed a system of Uranian astrology that had some cachet in Europe and that incorporated a series of hypothetical planets to fine-tune the traditional horoscope. I came up with a clutch of black planets swirling in a fire pit of malevolent angles. Jenny and I asked the surgeon to postpone the operation, making up an excuse about needing to visit Jenny's mother in Mexico. He gave us another date—and with the extra time performed one or two more tests that showed there was no third kidney after all and a much safer, simpler operation could be performed.

I was convinced astrology saved my daughter's life. And then I wanted it to save mine. Until then, I had used it to play with my own unhappiness. My life seemed to be adrift. On weekends or semester breaks, especially when old friends from Wisconsin passed through, I would waste days out by the Hudson River taking LSD and watching the riverbed become sheets of eels. When we went back to my house, I would dabble around trying to predict the future for us all. But the "miracle" that had rescued my daughter changed everything. I became obsessed with having to do my own chart.

I didn't know my birth time. There was nothing on my birth certificate; my relatives didn't know anything. I had to get my birth time. I became consumed with this. An accurate birth time was essential for calculating the Ascendant, key to the entire chart. There had to be a record somewhere. I went down to the Department of Health one afternoon and told them what I was looking for. When I showed them the birth certificate I had, the clerk explained that what I was carrying around was a standard short-form. There was a long-form certificate, she said, which I could also get. I immediately filled out an application and then waited. I remember the rush of excitement I felt when the clerk returned with the document. Only it did not have a birth time on it, either. In fact, I never should have been given it—it was a long-form certificate of birth by adoption.

The chain of coincidence that led step by step to my moment of discovery included blindness: clerical blindness, to be sure, but on a much deeper level an almost inexplicable and stubborn personal blindness that seems now, in retrospect, to have been present not only to protect me but more dramatically to demonstrate that will had nothing to do with what was about to happen.

2.

My mother lied to me that first time, flat-out lied. She held the long-form certificate in her hand, read it, digested it, told me without a second's hesitation that it wasn't what I thought it was, that I was my father's and her natural son and had been formally adopted only because I had been born out of wedlock. There was a kind of weariness in her tone that made what she said convincing. I remember feeling deflated—and then surprised—because I realized that I had really been looking for a Dickensian ending. It never struck me at the time (I felt too guilty) that I wanted to find out that I had different parents, at least a different father. I knew, for sure, that I *was* my mother's. My mother and I had the same wide face, brown eyes, full mouth, the same difficult nose. When my mother confessed to her agonies of living with a fat nose, my secret (well kept from her) was that I had spent years of my youth worrying about my nose, too.

It was different with my father, though. He was short, I was tall. My torso, limbs, features bore no resemblance to his. He had a different voice, different gestures, different nervous system. I had typical kids' fantasies when I was young that he wasn't my father. No one looking at the two of us together would have imagined we were related, whereas it was easy to see the resemblance between him and his other children.

My mother and I passed like ships in the night. She knew—because I asked her if she had any objection—that I wanted to look at my adoption record. I told her (and myself, too, because I could not bring myself to believe my mother would have lied to me about something like this so late in our lives) that all I was doing was tracking down my birth time so I could, at long last, finish my astrology chart. I didn't tell her anything about the hours I then spent at Surrogate's Court, about the different drafts of petitions to the court I was making to open my record—or about the fact that on some level I really didn't believe her. I didn't have to.

My mother, though outwardly calm, knew all this perfectly well. When I was around her and Harriet and Morty, I would get them talking about what it was like to have kept such a secret over the years. My tone was always light and ironic, as though I were more interested in being amused than informed. My mother knew better. She would disappear into another room while Morty, an amateur historian who was excellent with dates, would link different important events of the era—Kristallnacht, Roosevelt beating Landon—to milestones in the charade they had all been forced to keep going.

My mother was ready to give up, I think. The fight eventually went out of her. In retrospect, she must have hated having to keep up her cover story when she sensed I was already uneasy with it. When she finally caved in and told me the truth I became completely oblivious to her and what she might have been going through. I was interested in who she was only in relation to my real father—who turned out to be a movie star, a character who certainly fit a Dickensian ending.

What was he like? What did she know about him? Who was he? In my questioning of her, I feared that she really didn't know much about Van Heflin, that he was just a one-night stand, or maybe even that she slept around and someone else might have been my father and she had settled on him as the one because it best suited her fantasies. The closest to consciousness I could get to this question was dating the time of my conception. September 28—my birthday—minus nine months more or less led back to some time around New Year's Eve.

I pushed this out of my mind, however. I collected pictures of Van Heflin in which I could see the resemblances between us, between him and my son, Ivan (I overlooked the shots where there were none). I took note of every coincidence in our histories. There were many—and they were eerie. We were both six foot one, and had the same body type. There was the business of names (which my mother was well aware of). Ivan and Evan (my father's given name was Evan, shortened to Van). My mother's first and middle names were Eleanor Frances. Heflin's first wife was named Eleanor, his second wife Frances (same as his sister). I was amazed to discover that his first two grandchildren were named Benjamin and Eleanor, the names of my parents. When I saw this in his press clips, I was sure not only that he was my father but that he knew about me as well. Not so, said my mother (and, later, everyone in the Heflin family). One of the only clear memories I have of the aftermath of my discovery was when I asked my mother if my father knew about me. We were sitting outside on the lawn at Claverack late one afternoon. Harriet was sitting there with us. The day was clear and warm, shadows from the trees fell across the lawn, the surface of the pond was smooth as marble.

"No," my mother said, "I never told him about you."

I sat in a lawn chair opposite her. Harriet was sitting on the arm of my mother's chair. There was a moment of silence. I took in what she said to me. It was important, I knew, but I was confused by what I wanted and needed to hear. I didn't really believe her—but I wanted to, because I didn't want to hear that my father had rejected me.

"Why didn't you tell him?" I finally asked. My mother dragged on a cigarette and swirled some ice cubes around in the bottom of an empty glass.

"He was just starting to do well in his career—" She never finished her sentence.

Harriet burst out: "For God's sakes, Eleanor, I was in the room when you called him!"

My mother looked up at her sister, who was hovering over her.

"That's *not so!*"

"Eleanor, I was there!"

My mother got to her feet. "You weren't there, because it never happened!" The vehemence with which she said this got Harriet to her feet, too. But she didn't argue. Instead she shrugged and said, with a sad, quiet laugh, "If that's what you need to say," and she walked off, across the lawn and back to the house. I watched my aunt go, then sat there silently, unable even to look at my mother.

"What I told you is so," my mother finally said to me. I looked at her and nodded as though of course I believed her.

It would be many years—long after her death—before I could begin to sort out any of this for myself.

My mother only grudgingly talked about him. I felt I had to pry information from her. When she told me she met him in a theater group, she was so vague about it it took me a while to realize she was talking about the Group Theater. But I drank in whatever she said. I once asked her specifically what kind of person he was. She said—very reluctantly—she thought he was a decent person, very imaginative, and that there was something soft about him that other people could overlook. I asked her another time, point-blank, to describe the relationship she had with him: Did it go on for a while? Was it brief? What did she remember about it? My mother looked as if she were chewing on bad food. She shook her head. It didn't last long, she said. She shrugged and grimaced. She remembered giving him a gift once, a book. She took a beat and added that it was James Stephens's *The Crock of Gold.* The way she said this made me think she wasn't sure. In any case—at the time—it didn't seem important. Why that book? I wanted to know. I'm not even sure what her answer was— the book was imaginative, something like that—because mostly what she conveyed was the obvious distaste she felt in talking about anything to do with him. I concluded it was because she really didn't have much to say.

If my mother had her secrets, I had mine. I couldn't see clearly what my feelings were then. My birth father was a movie star and that was like the gift of a fairy tale I could live in. I could fantasize about him to the point where it became easier to turn away from my mother and all the difficult questions she raised for me—like why she and my stepfather had lied to me for so long, or why I could not begin to feel anything like anger for having had my history, my identity, my life betrayed. All I could think of was this missing father of mine, someone who had been dead for years but who, as far as I was concerned, was still alive and out there beckoning to me. It was as though my own sleeping ambition suddenly descended, like a sword, right into my hand, so I could raise it and go forth.

What my mother went through then never even registered. I didn't stop to think that the loss of her secret might have been as disorienting for her as the uncovering of it was for me. I never gave a single thought to the possibility that her secret had been her precious possession for forty years, that it might have all the while defined what she thought about herself—and about me. I could never have imagined that she might have looked at me and, because she so correctly surmised that I had turned my back on her and the family I came from, would feel that *she*, not me, was the one who had been stabbed in the back.

Van Heflin in Patterns *(1956)*
(Patterns © *1956 United Artists Corporation.*
All rights reserved.)

PART TWO

Shane

The homesteaders live in mud so deep they cannot dig graves
through it until spring turns to summer. Joe Starrett is the foundation upon which all this will be built. The woman who stands at his
side, wiping her hands on her apron, has surrendered her life to his. The
boy, their son, with a face round as one of Raphael's angels, panto-
mimes the killing of a prairie gopher or a luckless deer trapped in the
family's muddy yard.

One day, a stranger, a solitary rider, comes down out of the mountains. He is dressed in buckskin and there is a single pearl-handled revolver holstered on his hip. He stops near the doorway of the Starretts' cabin. Joe Starrett can tell from the stranger's first words that he has been bruised by killing and softened by nightmares. His nerves are gone. When little Joey Starrett cocks his toy rifle, the stranger whirls and levels his gun at the boy's heart.

The father offers the rider shelter in his log cabin. Marian, the wife, cooks for him; the boy shines in the dark watching him. Time passes. War breaks out—or at least murder. Cattle ranchers see the homesteaders as a threat to their grazing land. Rancher Ryker has a professional killer in his employ. This killer, Jack Wilson, draws on black gloves, smiles a death's-head smile, and provokes those he is about to kill to draw on him first. He murders one of the homesteaders, Frank Torrey, sending him hurtling facedown into the primordial mud. The message to the homesteaders is clear: move away and leave the range to the ranchers.

Instead, Joe Starrett rallies the homesteaders, pleads with them, cajoles them to stay and not let themselves be intimidated. With Shane at his side, he rides into town—with his starry-eyed son trailing after. When Starrett finds himself in the middle of a barroom brawl with the ranchers, Shane is right there with him. The little boy glowing in the dark has eyes only for Shane. But then, one day, when the killing has gone too far and the homesteaders are about to come apart, honest Joe Starrett decides that he must go into town and take on Rancher Ryker himself, even though he likely will die if he does. But Shane will not let him do this. The two of them quarrel—and then fight. Their fight, like everything in the movie, is epic and outsized, beginning in reality and ending in myth. Joe Starrett, simple, honest Joe Starrett, champion of his family and of all the homesteaders, becomes a whirlwind of clublike arms and tree-thick legs. Cries, screams, battle roars emanate from his body. He is Roland blowing his brains out on his horn. He cannot be *defeated other than by treachery. Shane, at the last moment, pulls a gun from his holster and cold-cocks Joe, who topples to the ground like that overturned tree stump in his yard. "I hate you, Shane!" cries the boy, who, in the end, discovers the love he has always had for his father—as well as for simple fair play. But Shane never was a coward. It is his destiny to make that ride into town, to stand in for Joe and all the homesteaders, to take out the man in black and Ryker, too, and then ride off into the darkness whence he came, so that the little angel-boy, who could not help following him, calls out, at the edge of the darkness, "Come back, Shane! Shane, come back!"—before turning around and going back across the desolate land to the warmth of his family and the world that has always nourished him.*

Shane
Paramount, 1953 (117 minutes)

TEN

1.

I turned my back on my mother and went out to find my father. I was obsessed by him. He had been dead for six years—his ashes had been scattered in the Pacific Ocean—but, to me, he was alive and waiting.

I looked for him first in libraries and movie theaters. His studio bio was the usual unreliable mix of press agentry and data. He was born Emmet Evan Heflin on December 13, 1910, in the farm town of Walters, Oklahoma. He was one of three children in a relatively prosperous family. The father was a dentist; the mother, from a well-to-do California family, was, in the words of the era, a homemaker. The family moved from Walters to Oklahoma City when he was one, but when he was a teenager his parents separated and the mother took the children with her back to California. Two of the children lived with her; he lived with his grandmother. Many years later, a friend of his told a reporter that his life then was hard and miserable.

Though he acted in school plays, he never thought about becoming an actor. He was attracted to the sea. On summer vacations he worked aboard fishing boats and schooners sailing out of Long Beach. When he graduated from school, he became a merchant seaman, eventually securing a third mate's license for himself. His favorite author was said to be Joseph Conrad.

He found his way to the theater—or, as his publicists had it, the theater found its way to him. While he was on layover in New York following one of his voyages, he auditioned for—and got—a small part in a short-lived Broadway play. Who knows if it actually happened that way. He did study seriously, however. He spent six months at the Hedgerow Theater in Pennsylvania and then got a scholarship to the renowned George Pierce Baker 47 Workshop at Yale, where he stayed for a year and got a master's degree in theater.

He was in New York for a while, appearing in one flop after another. In the late summer of 1935, he landed a good part in S. N. Behrman's play *End of Summer* with Ina Claire and Osgood Perkins. The play went on the road and opened in New York the following January. He wound up with star billing—and a trip to Hollywood. Katharine Hepburn liked him in it and had him cast opposite her in *A Woman Rebels*. Whatever relationship he had had with my mother must have ended just prior to this period.

He was not an instant success in the movies. After *A*

Woman Rebels, he did a slew of B-movies for RKO, returning to New York and the stage to star with Hepburn once again—in James Barry's *Philadelphia Story.* It was said by gossip columnists at the time that he and Hepburn were something more than friends. The play got my father back to Hollywood under contract to MGM, though James Stewart was cast opposite Hepburn in the movie version.

Van Heflin was an odd and different kind of actor in films. Through fifty-five movies, he was never really a leading man or a character actor. Said one critic, he was handsome in a homely kind of way (or maybe it was the other way around). He played tough guys, softies, rugged individualists, weaklings hung up on booze or unavailable women or careers that didn't work out. He could be solid and upstanding, a man of integrity, a good father and husband. But just as convincingly, he could be a weakling, a villain—and a madman. Who was he? Arthur Miller said my father reminded him of Arthur Kennedy. The two of them, he said, were wonderful actors who just didn't fit anywhere.

As the villain Rader in *Sante Fe Trail,* a confused and hokey film bio of the abolitionist John Brown, he looks the way my son, Ivan, does today. In *Johnny Eager,* his youthful looks are gentler. Playing a poetry-spouting drunk, he has watery eyes, and his strong chin seems subaqueous. He won an Academy Award as best supporting actor for this one. But his career wandered after that. War interrupted it for three years. He plays a believable drifter in *The Strange Love of Martha Ivers;* a drunken swashbuckler in *The Three Musketeers;* a rough-hewn adventurer in *Green Dolphin Street;* a nice-guy cop in *East Side, West Side;* the milksop husband in *Madame Bovary;* a rugged homesteader in *Shane;* a rancher in *3:10 to Yuma;* a conflicted executive in *Patterns.* He's a mad bomber in his last film, *Airport* (1970).

He had interesting things to say about acting. He told an interviewer once that he tried to imagine different animals for the roles he played. "I've been a Napoleonic dog, a panther, and a fat-faced owl," he said. Frank Sinatra referred to him once as "an actor's actor." I'm sure my father cherished that, but I have no idea what he actually thought about himself as an actor. Miller believed he was too self-conscious in the original stage version of *A View from the Bridge,* struggling over things like getting his accent right rather than focusing on the character's emotional life. He was too constrained, Miller said, and too passive when things weren't working in rehearsal. Overall, he never held together as a star. Like many actors, he wound up taking any part that came along. He was a drinker. He went through a bitter divorce near the end of his life and wound up living alone in one of those Hollywood apartment hotels Nathanael West wrote about. His death was sad. He was found unconscious clinging to the ladder of a swimming pool one morning, having suffered a massive heart attack. He never regained consciousness, though he lived a month longer.

I watched his movies over and over again. I could tell how much he longed for the child he never knew about in *A Woman Rebels.* I watched *Possessed* a second and third time because I didn't believe what I saw the first and second. It opens on a nearly deserted street in downtown L.A. at dawn. A woman in a daze, Joan Crawford, staggers out into the roadway to wait for an oncoming trolley. When the trolley stops and the doors open to let her on, Crawford looks at the conductor and says, "David?" She repeats herself. "I'm looking for David." She's in another world. She stops at a church, at a street corner, at a café, asking over and over again for David. Finally, she collapses and is taken to a hospital in an obviously psychotic state. She is given an injection, and the scene flashes back to the David she's looking for—my father.

I didn't need to pick my way through the different faces and costumes he wore. I didn't care if he was a fat-faced owl or a Napoleonic dog.

In *Shane,* his best movie, maybe he was a Kodiak bear when he played the part of Joe Starrett. He moved with a lumbering slowness that disguised speed and strength. But he was the perfect father. There were television series, *The Waltons* and others, that were spawned from his character. I watched the way he moved, his laborious, passionate manner, his clumsiness, his sweetness, his buried frustration and anger, which seemed always to be there just an inch or so beneath a pleasant exterior. I observed the way his hands wrapped around the handle of an ax or how he stood in the saddle, sat in a chair, took his food, raised and lowered his eyes. I watched how he uprooted a tree in his yard, how he placed an arm around his wife's shoulder, how gently he caressed the back of his son's head. Light fell across his face, shadows across his cheekbones, along the ridges of his temple and jaw, in such a haunting manner.

He was the one I was looking for.

2.

I thought I'd find Van Heflin in my newly discovered family, but I never did.

I first contacted his sister, Frances—Fra—who lived in New York. I wrote her a letter saying something to the effect that I had come across information that I thought might be of interest to her concerning her brother—something euphemistic like that—and followed this up with a call; she agreed to see me.

I felt like Pip at Miss Havisham's. Her apartment on West End Avenue was huge, dark, full of elegant old furniture, lamps, and knickknacks. I sat in the living room with her and her husband, who never said a word the whole time I was there.

I wanted at all costs to be accepted. I wanted this so badly she could have put a ring in my nose and led me around by a rope and I would have gone anywhere and done anything. I told her my story. She said, very quietly, "I thought it might be that." From the way she said it, I wanted to tell her it wasn't so.

She was small, had pale, milky skin, red hair, and watery blue eyes. She looked like him. Her voice was mild. Each question she asked—about my background, my parents, when and where my mother might have met her brother— came floating up out of this mild wash.

At one point, she showed me a room in her house that was covered with pictures of my father. There were publicity shots, snapshots, studio portraits. The only one I remember is a black-and-white portrait in which his face looms out of a background of dramatic lighting like that of Orson Welles in *Citizen Kane*. His eyes look crazy, angry, judgmental. I think there may have been pictures of his other children, too, but I am not sure.

She told me about the origins of the Heflin family. They had been in America almost since Plymouth Rock. One founding branch of the family was named Shippey, the other Bleecker (the New York Bleeckers, as in Bleecker Street). A Heflin married a Shippey somewhere along the line. The family was Dutch, French, also Scottish or Irish—and Episcopalian. I felt like Judas in my heart. My Jewish identity, in that moment, was gone with the speed of a card up a magician's sleeve.

She told me about my father's career and why it declined (he chose scripts badly). I was told about his children, where they lived, what they did. But she seemed indifferent when I asked if she thought they would be upset by my contacting them. All of us were past the time when we might connect as a family, she said, but there was no reason we couldn't be friends—if we liked each other.

At another point, she offered me a drink. I said no because I wanted so badly to impress her. "All Heflins drink," she said—very dramatically, too, I thought. I would have given anything to take back what I had said, to quaff down a full glass of one-hundred-proof anything. Instead, I just sat there and watched as she and her husband poured drinks for themselves. In a little while she got to her feet, letting me know it was time to go. It was all over, I told myself. She walked me out to the hallway and waited with me until the elevator came.

Visiting in Oregon with Tracy Heflin. Vana's children, Eleanor and Benjamin, are on either side of me; Maureen, in her backpack, is peeking over my shoulder.

But then, just before the car arrived, she smiled at me.

"Well, I'll tell you one thing, you certainly do have the Heflin hands, you can't lie about that," she said.

But after that I saw Fra only a couple more times. When I wanted to bring Jenny and the children down to meet her, she said she had no time during the week in the city (she was an actress on a soap opera), only on the weekends, when she and her husband went to their house in the Hamptons. I said we would be glad to drive out to see her and she tried to dissuade me, telling me it was much too long a drive. But I wouldn't take no for an answer. I made arrangements for us to visit. It took four hours to get there. Fra and her husband were moody, withdrawn, and seemingly distracted when we

arrived. It was clear we were not welcome. There was no food
laid out, no plans for dinner later. We spent a couple of awkward hours: we were shown through the house, took a walk
down to the ocean and back, and that was it. When we got
back, we got our things together and left.

The children visited Fra once on the set of her soap
opera, and I stopped off at her apartment one other time,
about a year later, to tell her I was thinking about making a
career change: I wanted to become an actor again. I went on
and on about how I had to return to what I knew was my true
calling. She probably needed to hear nothing else. From then
on, there were no more visits, phone calls, anything. I called
her once, I remember, and she actually hung up. "Fra?" I said,
when she answered the phone. "She's not in," the voice said.
But it was her. I never tried to contact her again after that.

I met and spent time with my Heflin sisters and brother
on only a handful of occasions over a couple of years. I contacted Vana, the oldest, first. I flew out to see her and Tracy,
the younger brother, who was staying with her at the time in
Oregon, where she lived. We made arrangements to meet at a
roadside restaurant near the airport.

When I got to the place, it seemed empty. I had this hor-
rible, sinking feeling that I had come three thousand miles for
nothing. Then I saw two people sitting in the back in the
dark. Vana looked up and waved—as though she knew me
and was glad to see me. The two of them stood up and we all
shook hands. I can still see the look of curiosity and vulnerability on Vana's face, the wide-eyed, open look on my
brother's—the face of my father as a young man. We must
have been there for an hour or so but, strangely, the only specific recollection I have is that Tchaikovsky's *1812* Overture,

with its smashing finale of cannons and great church bells, was playing on the restaurant stereo.

Later, at Vana's house, where I stayed, we talked ourselves into the ground. I showed them pictures of Jenny and the kids, I told them what I knew of my mother's story. They told me, in turn, about growing up in Hollywood, how the kids on the street where they lived were the children of other movie stars. Vana said she never understood this part of her childhood as different except that she felt she never quite measured up. She told me about her parents' divorce. Her mother had been having an affair with the best friend of the family, she said. It was all terribly ugly. I wanted to know what my father was like as a father. Tracy said he was too young to remember, because the divorce took place when he was a kid. Vana looked a little uneasy. Stern, she said; he had a temper. She remembered that once he objected to a date she was going to have—didn't think the boyfriend was right for her or something. He came out of the house after her when she was leaving for the evening, walked down to the car she had just gotten into, and ordered her back into the house.

The most vivid memory I have of that first night together was when we took off our shoes and socks and compared feet. The Heflins, Vana said, all had a peculiar cystlike protuberance of bone on the outside margins of their feet, and she wondered if I had that bone, too. I did not. Vana and Tracy sat there watching me as I peeled off my socks. I stared at my feet, which were as smooth as sausage casings. I remember leaning over and pulling the skin taut on the side of my feet to see if I couldn't come up with that Heflin bone.

The next day, the three of us, along with Vana's children, went hiking along the Columbia River gorge. We stopped and had a picnic lunch at a waterfall. Vana took a picture of me with Maureen, her youngest child, in a sling on my back, with her two other children, Benjamin and Eleanor, standing at my side, with Tracy just off to my right.

A couple of months later—that summer—Jenny, the children, and I packed up our car and took a camping trip to the West Coast. We spent a couple of days with Vana and her children in Oregon—sitting around campfires, swimming, and boating. Ivan and Ellen and Benjamin and Eleanor became playmates; Benjamin and Ivan swapped fishing poles. The very ordinariness of that time was what I most remember. But I never saw or talked to Vana after that. To this day, I'm not sure why; perhaps it was something specific, or just that the drag of living three thousand miles apart became a convenient excuse to turn off something that really took too much out of both of us. I wrote a couple of letters that went unanswered. I left messages Vana never returned. In the end, rationalizing what had happened, unwilling to look at the hurt I felt, I gave up trying to pursue her.

I also met my half sister Katie for the first time during that summer. After we left Oregon, we drove down to San Francisco, where she was working as a Tarot-card reader at a Renaissance fair. Of all the Heflin children, she looked most like my father, with flaming red hair, a wide jaw, and watery blue eyes. She was exuberant and theatrical. Her voice was low and husky—a perfect stage voice—and her dress and manner were flamboyant. We had known each other less than an hour when she playfully referred to me as "Brother David" and I quickly followed by calling her "Sister Kate." She did Tarot readings for us all, turning all the cards right side up so that there could be no negative interpretations.

Katie prided herself on living like a Gypsy. She had no address, no ties to anyone—including, it seemed, anyone in the Heflin family. She and her nine-year-old son, Gabe, moved around in a mobile home, a made-over truck. Her clothing tended to the antique, with lots of costume jewelry, showers of bracelets, raindrops of rings—she was a person, a spirit in disguise. She was the one Heflin offspring who had had a real Hollywood career. Her resume included movies with Sam Peckinpah; she had been married to (and divorced from) a son of Sheilah Graham's. Then, somehow, she dropped all of that. I never found out why.

We were there a few days. We went to Golden Gate Park, had a picnic, tossed a Frisbee around, took home movies; one afternoon, we went to Point Reyes and built a campfire on a gray, chilly afternoon. I have a photograph of all of us, in a culvert in an open field, with pine trees shrouded in mist behind us. We're standing around a campfire. My hair is blowing; I have one arm around Katie, who's wrapped in a Mexican blanket with a straw hat pulled down over her eyes. She's smiling and leaning against me. My other arm is around Jenny and Ivan, who is between us, looking up at me, sticking out his tongue; Maggie, looking glum, is huddled against Jenny. Ellen is standing next to Maggie, smiling at the camera.

I drank in anything Katie said about my father, though the picture I got wasn't anything like the image I carried around in my mind. She remembered that on her tenth birthday she wanted more than anything to have a horse. Her father made a big fuss about the present he was going to give her. He handed her a humidor filled with horse manure. She burst into tears. Then he took her by the hand, led her outside, and showed her the horse he had bought for her. That was his type of humor, she said.

When she was much older, after her parents' divorce, when she was an actress and he was living alone, she went to visit him one day at his apartment hotel when he had been drinking. She was wearing a minidress, she said, and as soon as he saw her in it he began raving. He chased her down the hall, shouting obscenities at her. I think she told me this story because she sensed how unrealistic my picture of him was.

After that West Coast trip, we exchanged Christmas cards for a few years, but I saw her only one more time—in New York, after I became an actor again. Then the cards stopped; then they resumed. She had been in a dark place, but said little more about what she had been through. The back of a card she sent was decorated with a rainbow and the sun flooding the sky with benevolent rays. The card was sent from Mount Shasta, a place she described as sacred. I don't know where she moved after that—we lost touch again. Today, we still occasionally surprise each other with a holiday card—as do Tracy and I—but it is now more than twenty years since I have seen any of them.

3.

Within a few months of uncovering my birth story, I was informed that I was not going to receive tenure at Brooklyn College, where I had been teaching. I had thought I had a chance. I had been hired not in spite of my career as an antiwar activist at Wisconsin but almost because of it. At the time the department had started a special adult degree program for police officers and the chairman, perhaps amused by the idea, thought that I might be a lively fit. In fact, I enjoyed myself. My teaching evaluations were excellent, I published articles in my field, but then the program ran out of funding and was dropped—and so was I. The chairman called me into his office one day to let me know. He seemed almost apologetic. I remember asking him if he had any advice about where I might apply for a new job. He somberly suggested places like L.I.U. or some of the community colleges.

I told Jenny I wanted to resume my acting career. To me, this was another way of looking for my father, and I thought it was a reasonable thing to do. She went along. She told me years later that she knew me well enough to know there was nothing she could have said or done that would have made me change my mind. And she was right. I certainly didn't think through the consequences of what I was about to do—much less understand that my father had nothing to do with it.

I began working while I was still teaching. I landed a part on an episode of *Kojak,* which was filmed in New York. As soon as the euphoria wore off and the work began, I realized what I was up against: the terror of not having acted in fifteen years. I couldn't sleep. I took pills to knock myself out and they didn't work. I showed up on the set feeling as if my eyes were fried and my body was lead. I was petrified I would blow my lines with the cameras rolling. I watched Telly Savalas float through his part. Before each of his scenes, he pinned pieces of the script to the backs of chairs, the inside of lamps, anything that wouldn't be picked up by the camera. When the scene was shot, he *read* every one of his lines. He hadn't been able to—or didn't want to—memorize anything. He was a pro, smooth as a figure skater. When I did my scenes, the whole set jumped before my eyes. If someone had held a TelePrompTer with oversized print right in front of my face I wouldn't have been able to read it.

It took me some time to get comfortable. In the first play I did in regional theater (*The Runner Stumbles* in St. Louis), I went blank on opening night. It was about ten minutes into the first act. I stood there in the center of the stage as though someone had removed my brain and replaced it with a siren I couldn't turn off. I thought I was going to pass out.

When I was cast as the lead in a national bus-and-truck tour of *Chapter Two* a few months later, I went sky-high in dress rehearsal the night before we were to open at the thirty-five-hundred-seat Norfolk War Memorial Coliseum. I was so upset I walked through an invisible wall separating one part of the stage from the other, into the wings, and back to my dressing room. The director came running after me, wanting to know what had happened. I told him I was sick and had to get back to the hotel. From the hotel I called Jenny in New York and told her what had happened and said that I couldn't take it, that I had made a big mistake becoming an actor and wanted to quit.

"You know what, David? I'm tired and I'd like to quit, too," she said.

"What do you mean?"

"Figure it out," she said—and hung up.

It didn't penetrate that Jenny was talking about our marriage. I was okay the next night, opening night, and I got stronger through the run. By the time I got back to New York nine months later, I felt like a trouper. I was doing exactly what I was supposed to be doing.

There was a hitch in all this, however. My father wasn't out there, and I wasn't just making a mid-life career change. Beginning in St. Louis, with that first play I did away from home, I began drinking. (I had never liked alcohol before.) The director of the play and I would sit around talking after rehearsals—with a bottle of wine between us. Eventually, I started buying wine to keep in my apartment. I drank wine exclusively—never hard stuff. I drank every day, with or without company. Sometimes when I was sitting alone, I'd think of my father and wonder if I was an alcoholic. Of course I wasn't. But I wished I'd been a wine drinker that first day I met my aunt.

My drinking continued after St. Louis and I became something of a connoisseur. I bought good wine, never cheap stuff (unless there wasn't anything else I could get my hands on that day). After a while, I couldn't get through a day without drinking half to three-quarters of a bottle. But because drinking never interfered with performing—I would never let myself go out on stage high—and because I always had my wits about me, I never gave a thought to what I was doing. Back then all I knew was that I loved the taste of a good red. I got my palette to the point where I could tell the difference between vintages.

I enjoyed myself out on the road, away from my family. I enjoyed drinking with other actors, sitting around telling stories. Wine made me bold. It turned out I liked parties, noise, companionship, and the fuss people sometimes made over me. From time to time (not often, but enough), I would wake up with a strange woman in my bed and not quite remember how she got there. None of this meant much, I told myself, it was all part of an actor's life.

But then there was a side of my life that made no sense at all. After I was working fairly regularly, making enough money to support my family, I began stealing. I couldn't fathom this. The urge was completely compulsive. I could do no more to stop myself than a horseplayer with a hot tip. It began in St. Louis. I walked out of a supermarket one day with a bottle of wine under my coat. I had had no plans to pilfer it. In the aisle where the wine was kept, it was as though my hand suddenly found its way to the bottle and whisked it into the inside pocket of my parka. My heart was pounding—with excitement—when I got outside.

It was strange. In New York, I was Dr. David. On the road, I was Mr. Hyde. I left my mark in towns and cities across the country. The nine months I was out on tour with *Chapter Two* were like a crime spree.

I was simply out of control, and it was a miracle I wasn't caught, prosecuted, and put away. I never hid what I was doing. Two friends of mine in the company knew exactly what I was up to, because I brought them into it. In city after city, town after town, we would go out to dinner—to the best, most expensive restaurants around. When the meal ended and the check came, I would have them leave and I would sit there for a few moments, poring over the bill; then I would get up, pretend to go to the restroom, and duck out, to catch up with my friends on the street.

I went into a wine shop one day in Kansas City. For some reason, the most expensive wines in the place were displayed on an open rack. I couldn't believe it. There were $150 bottles of Lafite-Rothschild laid out like duckpins. I looked around casually, then slipped a bottle under my jacket and walked out. I went back to the hotel where we were staying, found my friends, and gave them the bottle. But then I realized I had cheated myself: I went back to the shop and stole another.

I collected enough booty for one of the Crusades. I stole apparel, cosmetics, books, records, jewelry. I lifted a set of ivory chessmen in one store, in another a watch. In rainy, muddy Louisiana, I went into a department store in a mall one day. I trooped over to the shoe department, unlaced my muddy boots, shoved them under a seat, tied on a brand-new pair, and walked them right out of the place.

I went into therapy briefly at the time all this was going on, but got no help. The therapist would tell me that the value I placed on myself was no more than the price tag of what I stole. I was living in a dream world, he said. I didn't like the therapist, and I knew he didn't like me. But before I quit, I happened to meet a woman in his therapy group to whom I became very attracted—as she became to me.

Like me, she was in a long-term relationship. The first time we went to bed with each other, she told me she wanted me to father her child. I said no, but I was amazed—and excited. How could I do this? But how could I stop myself? I kept saying no, all the while more and more drawn in, intrigued, ignited by everything that was forbidden, eerie, inescapable that led to the feeling I was my father's son. She emphasized that she wanted to raise the child with her partner, not me. There would never be a commitment beyond making her pregnant. The depth of passion and disengagement gave me the sense that I was flirting with my father's soul. I kept seeing my friend—and resisting; seeing her and resisting. She told me once—as if she were the chorus in a Greek play, warning me—that she knew I was especially vulnerable because of what had happened to me, and even that made no difference. I was convinced I would not actually make her pregnant. And I know now that I did only when I was certain—not intellectually, but in my bone marrow—that I would have the same relationship with this child that my father had had with me.

All of that is long ago, nearly two decades past. The child from this union—a daughter—was told about me when she was seven. I have never met her, and never expect to. She knows (because her mother told her) that anytime she wants to meet me I will be there, and that is enough.

When she was conceived, I expected my life to explode. It didn't. I felt compelled to tell Jenny and my children what had happened, because I couldn't face the idea of not telling them. My family must have sensed my despair—and didn't desert me.

I told Jenny first. I picked her up from work one afternoon and drove her home during rush hour. I chose that moment because I knew I'd have to be looking at traffic, not at her, when I spoke. When the words finally came out my eyes were riveted on streams of brake lights stretching into the distance as far as I could see. Jenny pounded the dashboard of the car. I still could not bring myself to turn my head. Her words were sharp, angry, tearful. She said something about robbery. What robbery? I wanted to know.

"That was my child, you bastard! You stole my child!" But then, almost inexplicably, the angry words subsided, and there was prolonged silence, or so it seemed. When Jenny spoke again, her voice was measured and without rancor. She asked when the child was due and then said that I had to be prepared to take the baby into our family if the parents ever reneged and refused to care for it.

At the time, I couldn't begin to understand her reaction. I simply welcomed it as an unanticipated reprieve. It did not begin to dawn on me until years later, when our children were grown and out of the house, that this had little to do with forgiveness or acceptance. Jenny believed I was on the verge of a nervous breakdown and, as she subsequently informed me, was not about to be the one who pushed me over the edge.

My daughter Ellen was sixteen at the time and she, too, gauged her response to a fear that I was about to fall apart. She said nothing when I told her. When I hugged her she hugged me back—because, she said, she was that worried about me.

Ivan was angry. Years later, he said he could not understand why I would have told him anything when he was only fourteen. He said it made him feel what I was saying about loving him wasn't true and had nothing to do with him.

What I couldn't begin to admit to my children or to Jenny—even to myself—was how deeply I had come to believe that I was following in my father's footsteps. I wasn't. I was someone who had lost any sense of who I was, where I had come from, and where I was going.

I couldn't begin to see then that my deepest feelings had nothing to do with my father—with movie stars, Dickensian endings, or career upheavals—but with pure, unadulterated fury at having had my life, my birthright, so blatantly manipulated. The consequences of those feelings were in everything I did and, most of all, in what I did not do—which was to confront my mother, to demand an accounting from her or, at least, some plausible explanation for all that had happened, not when she was nineteen but afterward, over a lifetime, when she had the chance to tell me something and didn't. She, not my father, was the one who haunted me. And

I can say now that my inability to see came not from a deceptive play of light on a movie screen, or even from a defect in my own character, but from the simple and primitive fear that if I ever let my mother see what I was really feeling I would lose her forever.

ELEVEN

1.

From the time I was a boy, the usual style of communication in my family had been a kind of forced repartee—a mixture of sarcasm, criticism, and playfulness—instead of real openness. This worked especially well in commenting on the insults of the outside world. It reinforced a sense among family members that we were a besieged unit. In our family, as my brother was fond of saying, blood was thicker than water. But this style worked less well when it came to matters of the heart, where the absence of answers and the presence of strong emotion could provoke explosions of anger, gusts of sentimentality, or just plain confusion. There was always an assumption of love in our family—which was not unreal—but it was never separate from a tendency toward posturing.

There was no smoothing things over between my mother and myself. I did not trust her. I lost all sense of affection I had for her, my stepfather, aunt, uncle, all the relatives I had grown up with. I saw only their posturing. Also, the foundation of my own life seemed equally spurious. I had no past, only a future.

The dreams I had about my mother warned me and confused me. In one of them, she came rushing out of nowhere, a knife raised over her head. She was dressed in black, garments streaming behind her. She was the Queen of Night, ululating and berserk. In another, she was sick with indigestion. I asked her if she would be all right, and she weakly, dolefully replied that she would be if I stayed with her. As the Queen of Night she was the mad defender of a realm where death was doled out to anyone who opposed her. As the woman with indigestion, she was pitiable and vulnerable, turning to me for help. She was alone in the world. Husband dead, children grown up and moved out, one a felon in hiding, another—the one she turned to so plaintively—a middle-aged man with an identity crisis.

I did not know how to deal with her. After her secret was out, silences, awkwardness, and euphemism took the place of familiarity between us. I told my mother I had contacted my father's family, for example, but I did this craftily, asking her questions about Heflin's sister and then telling her about my meeting Fra the week before. I'm not sure I ever told her about meeting his children.

My mother, for her part, was inscrutable. One day, I took her to my house for dinner while we were still living in the country. We were driving along, not having said a word to each other in twenty minutes, when out of nowhere she suddenly burst out: "I was so damned arrogant!" I had no idea what she meant. When I asked her, she looked at me as if I were crazy.

I didn't like her, didn't want to be around her—and I'm sure she saw that. I tried to remain disguised. When I decided to go back into acting, I lied about the reasons. I told her about getting fired from Brooklyn, but then I went into a song and dance about how difficult it would be to find another academic job. I made it sound as though going back into acting were my last chance before welfare. Though I said nothing about looking for my father, I did tell her about seeing my old agent, Stark, and how excited he was about my story. In a gust of phony innocence I let her know that he wanted me to change my name to Heflin but that I had declined. I really liked the name, I confessed, however it just wasn't for me. My mother told me, quietly and icily, that if I took the name Heflin she would never speak to me again.

Who was my mother? Who was I? A lifetime's assumptions between us had been swept away. We went back and forth on the same old seesaw of routine, yet everything was different. Even though my family and I spent weekend days with her and my aunt and uncle in the country, and my mother often came to our house, conversation between us about the past simply stopped. When I wanted to know something, I would turn to Harriet and Morty, people who really knew nothing of what I was pursuing. I asked my aunt one day if she had ever met Van Heflin. She made the sourest of faces. "*Oh, please,*" she said, as though he had been a figment of my mother's imagination. I pushed my aunt. Aside from being in the room when my mother called him once, did she ever talk to her about him? Never, Harriet said. I asked her directly what kind of relationship she thought my mother had had with him. My aunt laughed. "You tell me," she said.

What I never could have foreseen was that the armed truce between my mother and me was actually a privileged time, unperceived by us both. It was the only period we would ever have really to talk to each other, to untangle forty years of deception—and it evaporated as quickly as a summer sunshower.

One night, I got a call from Harriet, who told me that my mother had been in an automobile accident and had been injured. My aunt's voice was panicky and tearful. It was a terrible accident, she said. The car my mother had been in had been broadsided, and she had been thrown from it unconscious. My aunt could barely get the words out.

When I got to the hospital outside Poughkeepsie, about a half-hour's drive from my house, it was the middle of the night. The hospital was on a hill, and its silhouette against the dark sky made it look as forbidding as a dungeon or a fortress. Everything seemed deserted—parking lot, surrounding street and walks. I ran up a short hill to the entrance. There was no one in the lobby. The hallways were flooded with fluorescent light. A security guard finally appeared, walking slowly along one of the corridors toward the lobby. I rushed up to him and told him that I was looking for my mother, who had been in an automobile accident and recently brought in. Where could I find her, I wanted to know?

Try the emergency room, he said, giving me a strange look.

When I saw my mother, I remember forcing myself not to turn away. One eye was completely closed and there was a swelling around it the size and color of a small eggplant. Her nose and mouth were caked with blood. Her one open eye made her look as startled as a bird that had just been shot in flight. Her head was bound with a turban of bandaging. She smiled when she saw me, and murmured my name. I took her hand and held it. "I don't think I'm ready for the photographers," she said with a weak laugh. I squeezed her hand.

That was the last moment of affection between us that I remember.

It turned out there were no broken bones, no major damage beyond a severe concussion. Still, her doctors were worried for a while. They held her for a couple of extra days of observation and had her evaluated in New York in the weeks following. All tests came back negative; the visible, gross signs of the accident eventually receded. But her symptoms lingered. She would get up from a chair and suddenly find herself holding on to something to steady herself. She had numerous headaches and from time to time would become disoriented. In conversation, she would frequently lose her train of thought. Those who talked with her would come to moments when they simply had to pause and wait for her to find herself again. She never got completely over the effects of her accident.

I don't know that there ever would have been an easy time to do anything to end the cold war between us, but her ongoing symptoms only fortified the chill.

After I moved back to the city and my working life as an actor began in earnest again, I became especially wary about sharing anything to do with my career with my mother—

unlike the first time I was an actor. Sometimes, Jenny and the children would visit her for dinner and I'd show up late because I was in class that afternoon, or out auditioning, or rehearsing with a partner somewhere. I would say almost nothing about any of that. If Jenny asked me how it had gone, I would say, "Okay," or, if I really had something to report, I would whisper, "Later," and I'd wait until I was sure my mother was out of earshot. I kept telling myself I didn't want to upset her.

When I landed my first regional-theater job, the one in St. Louis, it was Jenny who told her. We all had dinner together a few days before I left; my mother never asked, and I never said anything, about the play I was going to do. I told her only when I would be leaving and returning. I didn't like myself for being so obviously hidden, but I couldn't help it.

Shortly after St. Louis, I landed a lead in a production of *Mr. Roberts* in Chapel Hill, North Carolina. It was spring, a beautiful time, and I told myself I needed to be more forthcoming. I not only let my mother know what I was doing but invited her to come to North Carolina and see me. To my surprise, she accepted. She flew down one weekend with Harriet and Morty.

I was thrown off by her being there. We were in the second week of the run, and I was almost enjoying what I was doing. There were nights when I went out onstage and believed I *was* Mr. Roberts, that the exit sign in the back of the theater was the moon over the Pacific. When my mother turned up, the moon became an exit sign again.

My mother, though, was in her own world. After the performance, all of us—she, Harriet, Morty, Jenny, and I—walked across the university campus, where the theater was located, to the main streets of Chapel Hill. Jenny and my aunt and uncle had told me how much they liked the play and me in it. My mother hadn't said a word. Finally, walking at her side, I asked her what she thought.

"You weren't bad," she said. "I liked Henry Fonda better."

If she had said this before her accident, I might have made some retort, but now I couldn't bring myself to say a word. Instead, I trudged along silently, hating her. Later on, when she wasn't around, I mentioned what she had said to my aunt and Jenny. Harriet, for a moment, had a studied and serious look on her face. Then she burst out laughing.

That summer, when Jenny, the children, and I packed up our car and drove west to meet the Heflins, my mother went on a tour of Scotland and Wales with Harriet and Morty, stopping off at old inns, visiting castles and battlefield sites from the days of the Bruces. One night, my mother collapsed at a country inn where they were staying. It happened in the middle of the night, when no one was awake. Morty said she had gotten out of bed for some reason and fallen on the floor of her room. She was unable to get up, even to crawl. She lay there, apparently deciding not to call out—to wait for morning. My aunt found her hours later. They took her to a hospital, where a doctor gave her a cursory neurological examination and released her, urging her to see her regular physician when she returned home. The trip lasted another couple of weeks and finished without further incident. My mother decided she was all right.

But when she got back, she started to have symptoms she had not had before. She began to knock things over. One time it was a drink, another a vase, then a platter of food. Walking became more difficult. Her legs felt peculiar and unsteady. She became conscious, she said, of the way she stepped off curbs. One evening, in her own apartment, she fell again. No one was home, but she was able to pull herself up and get into bed. In the morning, she noticed that an area on her hip and backside was black and blue. She called my brother, who took her to the doctor that same day. After examining her, the doctor made arrangements for her to be admitted to the hospital.

My brother, Jenny, Harriet, Morty, and I had all gathered in her hospital room when her tests were completed late one afternoon. The room itself was quite attractive, on a high floor overlooking the East River, which at dusk was especially beautiful. My mother, in an elegant maroon robe, with her family at her side, looked like a movie star surrounded by a court of devotees.

When her doctors finally turned up with the results, my mother got up from her chair to greet them. The doctors, in their white coats, carrying clipboards, folders, and sheets of X rays, surrounded her. She disappeared in their midst, a tiny figure.

She was told she had an inoperable brain tumor—cancer (though the word itself was never used)—located on the exact site of the injury she had sustained in the car crash. They explained that surgery would be impossible, because it would mean cutting into a vital area of the brain. She would have to undergo radiation and chemo. The surgeon in charge of her case told her he was sorry to bring her such bad news and he seemed as crestfallen as everyone else in the room. My mother then asked him if he had anything more to say. No, the doctor said. My mother asked him to leave. When the doctors filed out of the room, my mother turned to us. There was something heightened and dramatic in her expression, almost as if she were aware of a moment at center stage.

"Well, I'll tell you one thing," she said, "this won't kill me!"

And she was right. The doctors made it clear that her chances of surviving more than six months were minimal. Statistics and percentages were cited. For a month, my mother received massive doses of radiation accompanied by a menu of powerful drugs. Her hair fell out, her face ballooned, her eyes became small as peas in the sacs of flesh around her cheeks. But she rallied. At the end of the month, she was weak but able to get around. In the months that followed, she had good days and bad days. When the weather was clear, she insisted on going up to the country. Harriet and Morty picked her up at her apartment and took her there and back. If she felt up to it, she went into town to do the week's shopping with Harriet. She cooked, cleaned house, sat around with drinks, cigarettes, the book she was reading, the Sunday *Times'* crossword puzzle.

Toward the end of the following summer, I don't know when exactly, my mother's friend Ruth stopped off in Claverack. She was preparing to move to the West Coast to retire. If my mother hadn't survived, this visit wouldn't have taken place. But there she was late one afternoon, sitting around on the patio with one or two stiff drinks in her, talking about the old days, about Duncan, the movement, my mother—and me.

Ruth, especially when she was lit, would frequently get sentimental, remembering me as a child. I enjoyed her but tended to fade away as her voice cracked, her eyes misted over, and she told me how lovable I was when I was two.

I don't know how many drinks she had had, but she was

My mother with my daughter Maggie (1980)

weeping and talking to her ice cubes. My mother was inside with Harriet fixing dinner, the children were outside, Morty was somewhere else. Ruth was saying something about the way I used to look. I was barely paying attention.

"Oh, yes," she said. "The first time your mother and I came to visit you in the home, your eyes were blue. We'd laugh and joke about it. Then—oh, God, I can still see you standing there like it was yesterday. We came to the home on your first birthday. The nurses had put balloons up over your crib. They had dressed you in a little sailor suit. Your face was so solemn." Ruth laughed and wept. "Your eyes were starting to change color!"

It was quiet on the patio. The late-afternoon shadows were deep and rich. The air was still. That was the first time anyone had said anything to me about my being in an orphanage.

2.

When Ruth realized that I knew nothing, she was appalled. She was sure I had been told, and even more certain that no one had mentioned to her that I hadn't been. I tried to assure her as much as I could that it wasn't a big deal—only because I wanted her to tell me more. What was the name of this place? Where was it? When was I placed there? How long did I stay? Ruth very shakily said she had only seen me there a few times and didn't remember too much—just that my mother had put me in and gotten me out before I was two. She pleaded with me not to make a fuss.

I collared Harriet that same day. Yes, it was true, I was in the Home for Hebrew Infants—for less than two years. I was there because my mother hadn't been sure what to do with me, Harriet said. I was taken out of the place because I was getting too old. My mother was informed that a decision had to be made about me—whether or not to give me up for adoption—before I was three.

Harriet remembered that the home was on Kingsbridge Avenue in the Bronx, had gone out of business long ago, and had since become an old-age home. Because I wanted her to keep talking, I made a lighthearted joke about maybe winding up there again when I was seventy. She said I was visited regularly, that the place was neat and clean—the best of its kind around—and that I was very well cared for.

Later in the week, I went to my mother's apartment near

Greenwich Village. When I got there, she was in a wheel-chair. She was having a bad day, her nurse said. She had been having a hard time walking, and she just wasn't herself. The nurse seemed upset.

My mother was sitting by the living-room window, look-ing out on Seventh Avenue. She turned and smiled when she saw me, but seemed to be in her own world. I pulled up a chair and sat next to her. I asked her how she was feeling.

"Been better," she said.

After a while, when the silence became too much, I finally said: "I found out about the orphanage. Do you want to tell me about it?"

I wasn't sure she heard me. She had a blank look on her face, as though I weren't there. She kept looking out the window.

"Do you want to tell me about the orphanage I was in?" I repeated. My mother's expression changed. Her eyes sud-denly seemed to darken and fill up, her lip quivered.

"It's over there," she cried in a loud, heartbroken tone.

She raised a shaky hand and pointed to a building across the way.

"*That's* the orphanage?" I said.

She nodded. Directly across the way was the old Mar-itime Union building, and farther down the street was the dark hulk of the old High School of Needle Trades.

"The school was . . . the orphanage?" I said, very slowly.

"Yes," my mother said, in the same tone.

I asked her nothing else.

My mother's condition spiraled dramatically. Soon after, there was a party of some kind at my brother's house. Harriet and Morty pulled up with her in their car, but it was almost impossible for her to get out and stand. Everyone in the driveway stopped and watched her emerge slowly from the backseat; the cotton-candy puff of her wig poked up first; her body laboriously followed, inch by shaky inch, a nurse at one elbow, my brother at the other, until she was upright like a stack of blocks about to fall over. Inside the house, she might as well have been a twig snagged in a stream. She said nothing. It was impossible to tell from her expression what she was thinking or feeling. Occasionally, one of her legs would begin to twitch. These spasms would last for a few seconds and subside. The only sign that she was even aware of them was a slight tightening at the corners of her mouth.

Shortly thereafter her doctors confirmed the obvious. CAT scans and other X rays still showed there was no return of her cancer, but one of the ventricles near the site of the tumor had, as a result of the radiation she had received, grown dramatically larger, creating pressure on the brain and destroying vital tissue. This deterioration was progressive and irreversible.

All too soon, she became wheelchair-bound and completely withdrawn. She retreated into an impenetrable and private world; it was unclear if she recognized anyone or anything, and communication was only about the simplest, most basic needs.

I spent the briefest time trying to research the orphanage I had been in, and then I gave up. There was scant reference to it in books and articles dealing with New York foundling homes of the period—and I didn't trust that my relatives would tell me anything.

One day, I took myself over to the premises just to have a look at it. I stood on the street debating with myself whether

I should go in, walking up and down in front of a wrought-iron fence, peeking in at a squat, red brick box of a building that looked more like a prison or an old hospital than a place where children had been cared for. Next to this building was a new, more modern-looking wing. There were old people moving around on the grounds, some in wheelchairs, some pushing walkers. I couldn't bring myself to go inside. When I got back in my car, I was done with my research. My mother was the only one who knew what I was looking for, and she was now beyond reach.

As her condition worsened, I saw her less and less. Whenever I did visit, all I could take in was her steroid-swollen face and the sweet-sick odor of illness that clung to her. I nearly always brought my family with me and used them to shield myself from her. I'd watch my children sit next to her wheelchair. They would talk to her, ask her how she was feeling. They would say what they were doing in school as though it were the easiest, most natural thing to do, and I'd envy them for the simple openness of their feelings.

Over time, everything I felt for my mother—the anger, the sense of injustice, even the memories I had of her when I was growing up—slowly drained away. When I came to visit her on my own, it was almost as if she weren't there. I would wind up talking to her nurses and forget she was even in the room. I remember how surprised I was one day when Harriet aggressively asked her—shouted at her—what she was thinking about, and my mother answered, in a whisper, "Hughes Avenue" (the Segal sisters' childhood home).

Many years later, long after my mother was gone, when I realized I wanted to write about her, I contacted the nurse who had spent the most time with my mother during her last years and asked what her impressions of her were then. The letter I got back, in part, said this:

> She never really needed things. It seemed as if her illness didn't affect her at all. Spiritually she was above all that and had accepted life as it was—crude. I honestly was surprised about her calm, her resignation, her stoicism. Her skin was fine like porcelain. She enjoyed caressing her black cat, listening to the opera on the radio and, of course she fully enjoyed smoking.
>
> One time I remember she got very upset. I was contemplating the pictures Judith had painted and I asked her why her daughter never came to visit her. She burst into tears. I didn't expect that. I never mentioned this episode again but I did like the paintings very much because of the wonderful colors and to cheer your mother up I'd say I liked her paintings more than Picasso. She liked to hear this expression but never commented anything at all.
>
> David, you were her favorite. One could tell it by the way she looked at you when you came to visit. During the time I was there you came several times alone and you gave her a lot of happiness. Your mother was very happy to have all of you but when you came alone it was very different—it was *transcendental* for her.

I never saw that. I was blind to her and to myself. I remember I came to her house one day before I was to make a trip to Japan. My acting days were just about over then. I was spending more and more time as a freelance writer, and I was going to Japan to begin working on a book. I sat next to my mother and told her this, even though I was sure the words meant nothing. I realize now that I did this because, in some remote part of my psyche, I had wanted her then, as always, to be proud of me.

Just after I returned from Japan three weeks later, I got a call at home one morning from my brother. My mother had just died. I immediately went to her apartment, but when I got there the doctor who had signed the death certificate had left. Funeral arrangements had been made. My brother and the nurse who had been on duty were having a cup of coffee. I went into the room where my mother was lying half propped up in her hospital bed. The shades in the room were drawn. There were no lights on, so it was hard to see her features clearly. I moved closer to the bed. My mother's eyes were only half shut, and her jaw was open in a rigid position. A thin wash of light from the other rooms glinted on the surface of her teeth. I stood there for a moment, wanting someone to come in and close her mouth and eyes. I couldn't do it myself. I turned around and walked out of the room.

I'm not clear about who attended the funeral. I can remember that in the small, half-filled chapel, with its cream-colored walls and spare furnishings, there were my brother's family, mine, Harriet and Morty, and the small, round, grief-stricken face of my mother's cousin Harold. But that's it. It was decided that I would give the eulogy. I don't know who asked me, and I don't recall a word I said. The gist of my remarks, I'm told, was that my mother was two different people—the person everyone saw, especially in her last years, and the person she really was. I am told that people were moved by what I said, but I can't imagine why they would have been.

My mother, in reality, *was* two different people, but not as I meant it then. She was herself throughout her life, before and after her illness. She was another person only in what she kept hidden. I kept to the back of the small huddle of people who later gathered at the gravesite for the burial next to my stepfather. A thought flashed through my mind as I watched the casket sink out of sight: there were no more secrets between us.

But that was only because I was still blind.

TWELVE

1.

Years passed. I did not think about her. My life changed. I left acting. My children grew up, moved out of the house. I became a grandfather. My body or my drinking began to get the better of me. I collapsed one day and after lots of tests had to have a pacemaker installed. I was told I had to give up drinking. And in 1994, ten years after my mother died, Jenny and I, though we might have done this years before, decided it was time to separate. I began living alone when I was fifty-nine—about the same age when both my mother and father came to this experience in their lives.

Living alone. Ivan and Matthew, Ellen's husband, helped

move me into my new apartment, but when they left I felt like a trapped animal. I found every excuse I could to get out of the house. The daylight hours were bearable but not the night. During the evenings I stayed away until it was as close to bedtime as possible. I would look out my window at other apartments, at the rows and rows of darkened windows after midnight. It comforted me to know that lights were going out, that it was time for bed.

I began to think about my mother and father and what living alone must have been like for them. They became a kind of focal point for me, especially late at night. I conjured up images of them. I would try to imagine my father nursing his bottle in that apartment hotel room of his in Hollywood; I would see my mother sitting by herself in her living room.

That was when I realized that something had changed in the way I thought about my mother. One night, after I had been out and come home, I was making a cup of tea when I suddenly had this sense there was someone in the apartment with me. I knew who it was—instantly. I walked through the apartment, down the hallway to a rear bedroom, opening and closing closets. When my tea was ready I sat in the living room thinking about my mother.

I closed my eyes, trying to visualize her. I had trouble, because all I could conjure up were images of her at the end of her life, moon-faced and slumped in her wheelchair. I deliberately tried to reconstruct her face as that of a younger, healthy person but couldn't do it. It was like trying to piece together an extinct language. Then I remembered that I had a carton of family photos sitting in the hall closet that I had brought over to my apartment when Jenny and I separated. I got the box out of the closet and spread the pictures out on the living-room floor. I spent the rest of the night going over them.

There are hundreds of pictures—some, of unidentified people in my mother's and stepfather's families, dating from the last century. The oldest photos are sepia-tinted on hard backing and have Cyrillic lettering on them. All the subjects are staring stiffly and formally at the camera, so that you can almost visualize the clunky box facing them, the photographer stooped over with his head turtled under a cloth, arm upraised.

There are pictures of my mother's family: her mother and father, their parents, her mother's sisters, all the other relatives. There are pictures of my great-aunts Rose and Lee, probably from the 1890s. There are pictures of my grandparents when they were as young as my children.

There are pictures of my mother as a little girl, older girl, young woman, all the way through to the end of her life. In nearly all the early pictures of my mother with her sisters and friends, she is full of attitude, either mugging for the camera or hugging the friend or sister sitting in front of her. There is one of Nancy, Harriet, Hilda, my mother, and Harold, all standing in a stack from tall to small, Harriet wearing a huge white bow in her hair, smiling pleasingly at the lens, my mother with dark bangs, a mischievous curl to her lips, leaning toward Harold, who stands stiffly erect, in a white short-pants suit, like a miniature grandee.

There is one of her in her early teens, a formal study airbrushed and tinted, part of a set of portraits including her parents and sisters. Her face is a delicate oval, chin round, mouth wide, eyes large and dark, her expression serious but gentle. Her shoulders and neck are visible. She is wearing a demure-looking blouse with a wide, scalloped collar of white trim; a locket of some kind on a thin chain rests below her bare throat. She is a girl on the verge of womanhood. There is an extraordinary vulnerability in her look—she is a beauty, a striking, original beauty.

I went through picture after picture: my mother alone, my mother with each of her children, with my stepfather, her parents, with Harriet and Morty, my mother as a young woman, a middle-aged matron, an old woman in her wheelchair. The arc of her life was there, all of it. I was left with what I began with: a picture of my mother's pumpkin-shaped face and broken body, eyes staring dumbly at me. I felt a weight on my heart, a tearing of something deep and old, like the breaking free of barnacles from the side of a sunken ship. I was crying.

It is said that grief can be delayed. The abundance of literature on the subject makes clear that this is an individual process, but it is common, in the face of overwhelming loss, to shut down, to give oneself time to digest what has happened. The closing down or numbing, according to the British psychologist John Bowlby, is an inevitable stage of the grief process, one of several, leading to an ultimate acceptance of loss. But Bowlby and others believe numbing occurs immediately following a death and usually lasts for a relatively short period—days rather than weeks—and is then followed by a phase of intense yearning and searching. It is unusual for numbing to go on for ten years, still more unusual for spirits to interfere and jerk someone out of the numbing process. There are no studies that support my experience.

I worry about saying this. Even though I am an ex-astrologer, I am, as my mother once characterized me, a fairly

My mother, age seven, is in
front of Harriet (at right).

At age twelve (right), with
an unidentified friend

At age thirty

Eleanor Segal Siff,
1915–1984

With me (right) and Daniel in
the 1940s

In her Brontë days

With my stepfather, 1973

With Judy on October 18, 1981,
twenty-eight months before her death

conventional person. I am aware that I live in a time that is drunk with visitations from "other" worlds. Aliens invade us, kidnap us, take over our bodies. Polls indicate that up to three-quarters of Americans believe in the reality of angels. There is a flourishing "science" of angelology which, according to Harold Bloom, is a sign of our own decadence and diminished imagination.

My mother's spirit was troubled and ambiguous, not nearly so clear or stripped down to essentials. I have no idea why she appeared to me then, but I know she was restless, impatient, and even distracted while I went through those pictures. We began a conversation—without words—that went on for many years, and that led me, in the end, to the discovery that had eluded me my whole life.

Among all the pictures laid out on the living-room floor, I noticed that there were none of her around the time I was born, nothing in the years immediately preceding or following. This gap was strange, and I puzzled over it for a long time. On one side of the gap was that haunting portrait of my mother as an early teen, on the other side a handful of snapshots from around the time I was brought home from the orphanage. Then there was another puzzle. In those post-orphanage pictures, there were none of the two of us together. Was it because my mother didn't want to be photographed with me, or because no one thought to take a picture of us together? There is one in which she is standing on a rooftop alongside Harriet. I'm standing between them, looking pudgy and disconsolate. Though the top of the picture is cut off at the nose level of the women, I can tell who they are by their smiles. My mother's is crooked, brittle. There is another (taken no doubt the same day; I'm wearing the same outfit), where she's in a line of women—Harriet, Harriet's friends, and Harriet's mother-in-law. She is smiling, but her expression is tension-filled. Her hand is in her hair as if she's trying to hold a hat in place—but she's not wearing a hat. I'm standing like a solemn little drum major right in front of her.

I began talking to other people about my mother again, something I hadn't done in years. I did with my children, with Jenny (whenever I saw her), with friends, relatives, and, ultimately, strangers. I had seen Harriet and Morty less and less over the years, but when I did I always steered the conversation around to my mother.

I went over the same ground with them that I had years before. I wanted to reconstruct a history. What was it like growing up in that family, what was my mother like as a child, as a schoolgirl? Why did she get thrown out of school, where did she go, what did she do? I listened intently until I could feel my mother's presence in that life long ago. My aunt and uncle never said a harsh word about her, but they didn't have to, I could feel it. I could feel the old resentment my mother lived with in her home, the love and the censure both, the bewilderment on both sides as to why she was the way she was. My aunt was no longer fully in control of her faculties. Her mind, once sharp, had been slipping for years. Memory and focus were gone. Sometimes she would say things without really being aware of what she said. When I again asked about the part of my mother's life when she met my father, Harriet shrugged. There was silence and then, suddenly, she blurted out, "Your mother wasted her life." When I asked her what she meant, she looked uncomprehendingly at me. She had already forgotten what she'd said.

I went down to Washington, D.C., one day. Harold lived

there, as did my mother's old YPSL friend Florence Rossi. They were both surprised to hear from me. I hadn't seen or talked to Harold since my mother's funeral; it had been longer than that since I had seen Florence. I explained to them I was thinking about writing a book about my mother's life.

It was summer. The weather was typically steamy and uncomfortable. Harold's house was air-conditioned, and dark because the shades were pulled. We sat in a corner of his living room where there was light. He was in his early eighties and still sprightly. I could see the face of the little boy in the photo of the stack of children. As he talked, I had the sense that my mother was sitting in the room with us.

The two families—his and hers—were fungible, he said, they went everywhere and did everything together. They were neighbors in the city, they went to the same resorts during the summers, they once acted in the same summer play when they were at Pioneer Youth Camp, something called *Six Who Waited While the Lentils Boiled*. They were at a resort in Pennsylvania when President Harding died. They stood side by side, elbowing each other, during a memorial service for him given at the resort's bowling alley. And so on.

But Harold knew nothing about the time when my mother met my father, either. He was a young man just starting college then, and his friends were other young men. Though he saw my mother when she was pregnant (he had that job delivering medicines to customers on Park Avenue), all he could remember was that she seemed to be holding up and that he felt for her at a time when the whole family seemed consumed by the calamity that had befallen her.

Florence talked about my mother's seductive power back

then. "I don't know what the right word for it is," she said. She told me a story: "There was a guy by the name of Ernie Dorfler who was a little older then we were. He lived on Clay Avenue. Everybody was very poor, but I think his father owned the building, so I think he gave him an apartment for free on the top floor, and Ernie had a vast collection of books, from floor to ceiling. One of these books was a famous study of sex by Krafft-Ebbing. Eleanor wanted to read it, so she concocted this thing and dragged me along with her. I was an innocent dupe—anything she did I just followed her. We went up to the roof of the building when the Dorflers weren't home, went in through a window, and read Krafft-Ebbing so we could learn about sex."

Florence, however, was not in touch with her during the time when she was hanging around with the Group: my mother had broken away from the YPSLs by then. Florence said she first heard about my mother's having an illegitimate child later, from "some of the boys." She was even more surprised when I told her the name of the father. She was sure the father was someone my mother was reported to have been involved with from the Yiddish Art Theater. But she didn't remember the name of this person; she didn't really have firsthand information of any kind, she said. She next saw my mother—and me—when she visited my grandparents' house a couple of years later.

Florence remembered the names of some of the people who had been in Circle 8 of the Young People's Socialist League, when my mother was a member. Several of them were still living in the New York area. I looked them up. All of these people were in their eighties, one of them a philanthropist and retired millionaire, another a retired government worker, another an ex–union organizer. All of them remembered my mother. Murray Nathan recalled that he was one of at least three who had a crush on her. One of them was really in love with her, he said, and my mother sidestepped him by concocting a story about her being a lesbian. Another Circle Eighter, Harold Goldstein, remembered visiting my mother regularly at her home, "because we had such a good time there. She had almost what you could call a salon. She seemed to a seventeen-year-old to be the quintessence of sophistication. We didn't have liquor, we didn't have anything—except cigarettes and each other." All of them stressed how serious they were about their politics, and how surprised they were to hear about my mother's trouble. That sort of thing just did not happen then, even in radical circles. But these old friends knew nothing. My mother, at that time, had drifted away from the YPSL.

My mother's closest friends from that era, Ruth Fletcher and Max Rosenberg, also knew little. Ruth was on tour with her dance company when my mother met my father. Max had only sporadic contact with her, but remained close in the years immediately following. I dropped in on Max during one of his recent business trips to New York. I think my mother must have been hovering nearby, checking up on the two of us. Sitting in Max's fancy midtown hotel suite, I could almost see her there, arms crossed, a deep scowl on her face. I was edgy and on guard the whole time. We talked for awhile about her *saison*. "Happened to one other YPSL girl I knew. They went nuts. Their gonads or whatever." He knew about other scandals and troubles in the family. "Something happened to Ellie around that same time with that wonderful uncle who interfered with her. I'm talking about making sexual interference. Ellie must have been sixteen, seventeen already, and what's her name, the precise wife, the social worker, with the pince-nez and the rest of it, and Docky, that fucking guy with the bald head, he did something terrible to her—though I don't believe he succeeded."

He knew her when she was kicked out of school. "And that was a big disgrace, because Jewish kids just didn't get kicked out of school," he said. "It was a big trauma—and she was very upset about it, make no mistake."

And he knew her after the scandals were over, when, overnight, she became, in his words, a matriarch and the "spark plug of the family." He lived just a building away when I was growing up; he knew my mother after she reinvented herself, so he could put two sides of her life together: "You were a thorn in Ben's side and that just killed your mother," he said. "Everything he was good at you were bad at: he was a first-rate mathematician and you hated math; you didn't give a shit about school, he loved school. And everything you were interested in he hated. There he was—and your mother was just crazy about you. And Daniel became Ben's son, in effect his firstborn son, and Judy was his special love. You had a battle with him every day when you were five and six and seven and eight. It must have been a tortured and terrible time."

But all he could say about that missing passageway between the two sides of my mother's life was to call it craziness. He wanted to make sure I understood that the person he knew was different from—and more substantial than—the one who had disappeared for a year. "Ellie was never wild," he assured me. My mother quietly harrumphed in the corner when he said this.

Precisely because no one really knew about that time in her life, I knew I had to find out about it. I could almost hear my mother whispering that to me, telling me to keep going, not to settle for words like *saison*. But how could I find out more? Who knew my mother then, who were her friends, what were her dreams, what did she tell herself about what had happened? When I thought about it for myself, when I tried to picture my mother, I was caught in other people's images of her.

Harriet, Morty, Harold, my mother's friends present and past, all had views of her that were different from any I had. Daniel and Judy—free from her troubles with the law and with their own families now—would share stories about growing up. I had a framed picture on my desk of my mother and stepfather together on vacation, both of them looking happy. I found myself drifting away from time to time, talking to this picture, listening for answers that never came. I kept thinking about the part of my mother's life I had missed because she had been in hiding and I had been blind.

I tried to imagine what it was like for an eighteen-year-old girl to be on the streets in the midst of the Depression, a rebel girl with her coat buttoned up the back, believing and disbelieving that a new world was right around the corner. I tried to feel my way into her worrying, into that silent, gnawing uncertainty she had about her intelligence, her talent, her nose. I tried to imagine the excitement of the time. January 1935, Civic Repertory Theater, 14th Street, the Group is premiering *Waiting for Lefty*. The old, decaying 14th Street barn is packed to the second balcony. From the opening moments of the play the connection between the actors onstage and the audience is immediate and electric. There are shouts from the audience to the actors as the play progresses. At the play's climactic moment the shouts become a memorable rising up, a thousand-throated chant, "Strike! Strike! Strike!" I could almost feel what my mother was feeling, the joy and pain in her throat, the cold, thrilling storm of goosebumps on her arms. Was Van Heflin there with her then? Did she hug him at that moment, or reach over and take his hand and hold it aloft with hers?

That is when my mother knew him, when the plainest of worlds had been transformed, and when no one—family, friends, comrades from the movement—was able to offer her the kind of support or understanding she needed most.

How in the world was she supposed to carry through, supplying herself with a sense of clarity and acceptance that others did not have? How could she have avoided seeing what had happened in terms of scandal, damage, injury to everyone? This was the reality that had been forced on her. Wouldn't a young girl, in that situation, have finally come to turn on herself, to condemn herself with words like "foolish," "shameful," maybe even "arrogant"?

Trying to live in her skin, I could sense what it must have been like to hear her relatives, day after day, telling her how important it was for her to give up her child so she could get on with her life. I could see the expressions of concern on the faces of her mother, aunt, sister, hear the drumbeat of their heartfelt words that made her understand that these people only wanted the best for her. Whatever she did, whatever choices she made—holding on to her baby, giving him away—there was no way out. The more she relied on those who, out of love, condemned what had happened to her, the less there was of herself, the more there was of a disproportionate sense of obligation on the one hand, and equally intense shame and guilt on the other. The only one left to support her was herself.

Of course she would have tried to keep that secret. In her skin, imagining what she felt, the confusion that pulled at her like a riptide, I could bring myself to the moment when she surrendered her own child. I no longer cared that she had kept all this secret for so long, that she had had to lie to me, maybe even to herself, to hold on to that smallest yard of advantage for herself. I wasn't even sure that the story she finally told me was true. But it no longer mattered. Whether or not I was conceived on one drunken night, even if someone besides Van Heflin was my father, even if her reasons for surrendering me were conflicted and confused, my mother had done all she humanly could to make a life for herself—and for me. What more did I need to know?

My mother and stepfather smiled at me from the picture on my desk.

2.

Nineteen ninety-seven. Three more years have passed. Ellen; her husband, Matthew; and my grandson, Benjamin, have moved to Maine. Ivan has moved to Massachusetts. Maggie has graduated from college and is an actress. She is on the verge of winning a Barrymore Award for her role as the housekeeper who discovers that she is the illegitimate daughter of Captain Alving in a Philadelphia production of Ibsen's *Ghosts*. Jenny and I have made a kind of peace with each other so that we can still share our family and, occasionally, even go to a movie together. We're both still single, both living alone. I like living alone now. I belong to a good recovery program which has kept me at a distance from wine (and also soaks up some of the deadly evening hours). The past is the past. What has changed in three years is the absence of contact I've had with my mother's family. I rarely hear from any of them or they from me.

So it was a surprise when Morty called me one day. I had no idea how long it had been since I had seen or spoken to him or Harriet. I had heard—because my brother had told me—that they were selling their apartment in New York and moving to Washington, where their children lived. I felt a rush of guilt when I heard my uncle's voice on the phone.

But the call had nothing to do with the state of relations between us. My uncle said he was cleaning out his closets and had come across a folder of my mother's writings. He wanted to know if I wanted them—otherwise he was going to throw them out. Of course, I said. I was excited—and confused. I had no idea what kind of writing he was talking about, and I wondered what he was doing with anything of my mother's. I told him I would come down to pick up the folder right away.

When I got to their apartment, the folder was sitting on a low coffee table in the living room. It was marked, in black, smeary crayon in my stepfather's hand, "El's Wrtg." Morty said he must have cleared this out of Claverack after my mother had died and forgotten about it. I didn't know what to say. I kept opening and closing the folder to see what was there. I didn't want to be rude, but I couldn't help myself. I thought what I was looking at was a collection of old school papers from the time my mother was at Columbia. We spent an awkward half hour together. I was sure they could see how eager I was to leave. When I said goodbye, I hugged and kissed each of them. I felt a sudden rush of sadness. I knew that my aunt again would forget I had been in her house five minutes after I left.

As soon as I was out the door and in the hallway, I began to go through the folder. The top piece was my mother's Columbia master's thesis on the Brontës. There was another school paper—and a batch of short stories I had never seen, never even knew existed. The addresses on the cover sheets were all different, representing the different places where we had lived over the years. I looked greedily at the opening paragraphs of each of the stories as I waited for the elevator. Then, when I got home, I went through all of them the way I had gone through that box of photographs.

I had a mixed reaction to the stories as stories. None of them were really complete. As fictions, they were too thinly disguised. But because of that I could recognize my mother trying to deal with her own life in them. In one story, a daughter comforts a dying father in the hospital. The father is an aging immigrant and is treated condescendingly by his nurses. The daughter bridles at this and adoringly remembers how the father read great books aloud at the breakfast table. An old woman in another story, a widow, never complains about her hard life. Her memories go back to the Russia she left as a girl—and to what her life became in the New World. She recalls the untimely death of an adult child, she carries on conversations with her deceased husband about the child they lost, the failing store they operated, the friends who once surrounded them and made the walls of their house shake with laughter and talk of politics on Friday nights, "Pinochle night."

There are stories about children and the complex relationships they had with their parents, the rivalries they had with their sisters. There's a coming-of-age story about a young girl with an irrepressible and vivid imagination and a profound sense that something in her life is missing. Then there's one about a trapped housewife—the focus of the husband's life is his job, and the wife is isolated among a group of other trapped housewives who drink together but who cannot begin to open up to one another. The only part of her life not covered in her stories is that missing period—when I was born.

Then I read her school paper on the Brontës again. I remembered it for her picture of Charlotte Brontë's anger. But now, knowing her secret, I could also see clearly how much she was writing about love.

She portrays Charlotte Brontë as a woman who was never fulfilled in love. Early in her life, when she was a schoolgirl in Belgium, she fell in love with a schoolteacher, an older, married man named Heger who rejected her. My mother gives far greater emphasis to this episode in Brontë's life than Brontë scholars do. She includes the texts of many of the youthful letters Charlotte wrote to him, letters full of pain and longing, and adds, as commentary, a psychological explanation for how a woman's love can be inflamed by a man's inability to reciprocate. There is also a picture—again given too much emphasis—of Charlotte's late marriage to a man who was devoted to her but for whom she could feel only respect and gratitude. Hovering over the facts of Charlotte's life were the passionate creations of her imagination, especially the buried but redemptive love of Jane Eyre for Rochester.

This is what my mother wrote:

> In *Jane Eyre*, however, which was written when the Heger dream was over, all the abundant passion of Charlotte Brontë burst forth and flooded its pages. Jane's feelings are never restrained, they are stated copiously, torrentially. Her confession of love to Mr. Rochester is a startling departure from Victorian modesty. She is the aggressor and the first to declare her preference. What is even more remarkable is that love speaks through Jane in the accent of rage.

Once again, there was that missing piece of my mother's life—and mine—staring at me in the face. What was I supposed to think? Why was she goading me about that now? What was she trying to tell me that I didn't know already? I didn't want to carry on this conversation, but I could almost feel my mother telling me her papers had been turned over to me for a reason, so I could do something. But what? There was no answer, only a pulse in my brain. More in exasperation than anything else, I picked up the phone one day and called the old-age home that had been the orphanage where I had been left as an infant.

I remembered that I had once shied away from the front gate of the place, and so I thought I would make arrangements to have someone show me around. But the woman I spoke to on the phone was puzzled. She had no knowledge of the home's ever serving as an orphanage and seemed dubious when I said I wanted to come over and look around. I wondered if someone else might be willing to help me, but she couldn't think of anyone. I asked if I could speak to the director. No, she said, she was sure he wouldn't be able to help me, either. But I persisted. I got his name from her and then kept calling back until he finally—with a good deal of irritation—tried to brush me off.

What, precisely, did I want to know? he asked, tartly. I explained that as an infant I had been in the Home for Hebrew Infants and that I was writing a book about this, about my mother, and wondered if I could just come over and see the place. He said he was aware that there had once been an orphanage on the grounds but that was long ago, before he was born. What did I think he or anyone would be able to do for me? I told him I didn't know, that maybe just walking around and looking would trigger an old memory or two. He reminded me—emphatically—that the orphanage had gone out of business over fifty years ago and was sure that nothing there would remind me of anything. I asked him if he would just be willing to have someone show me around. He snapped that he and his staff did not have that kind of time.

"Call JCCA, see if they can help you," he said.

"JCCA?" I asked.

"Jewish Child Care Association," he said—and then hung up.

I followed his suggestion and got the name of this organization out of the phone book. It was a clearing house for many different social-service agencies affiliated with the Federation of Jewish Philanthropies. No one at this clearing house seemed to know more than the director of the old-age home. I kept getting shifted from extension to extension.

Finally, I spoke to someone in the Office of the Coordinator of Quality Assurance. The person who got on the phone tried to be helpful as I told her a little about my mother and myself. She referred me to a book that had a chapter on the Home for Hebrew Infants. I told her I had already read it. Wasn't there anything else I might find, maybe a record, or the names of some people who might have worked there once? She didn't think there would be much, beyond the book she had mentioned, but she took my name, said she would try to help, and told me to call back in a week or so. When I did, there was a big surprise waiting for me.

"We located a record," the coordinator said, speaking so excitedly it was hard to follow her. She used terms like "needle in a haystack," "totally unique," "unlike anything" she had seen. "We have a complete record of your time at the Home for Hebrew Infants," she said. "It's not their record, it's ours, and it covers everything. Your mother was an amazing woman," she said, "and I'm proud to have met her."

3.

The record turned over to me on December 16, 1997, covered a period in my mother's life from July 1935, almost three months before I was born, to December 1936, when I was fifteen months old. It is an eleven-page, single-spaced report, highly unusual in length for record keeping in that era. Across the top of the first page are the words "Jewish Children's Clearing Bureau." On the upper left-hand side of the document is the pseudonym "Stone." On the right-hand side of the page is the case number—9546. The narrative, as far as I was able to determine, was composed by one writer, a caseworker. The prose, consistent throughout, is formal and matter-of-fact, almost bureaucratic in tone, but just because of that is exceptionally focused on my mother's pregnancy and its aftermath—the missing period in her life I had been searching for.

The narrative opens with a furtive phone call to the bureau—from Harriet. She asks—nervously, the writer thinks—about finding a temporary boarding place for a child soon to be born who would then be placed for adoption. The writer/caseworker invites Miss Segal (Harriet) to come into the office to talk further.

Harriet, well dressed and very nervous, shows up a couple of days later and explains that the woman in question is her sister and that she is presently living apart from her family at an apartment in New York. Everything must be held secret—no records are to be kept, word absolutely must not get out, lest it injure her father, a druggist, "who was very well known" in his community. When the caseworker asks if it would be possible to visit the young girl in question, Harriet says she thinks so but cautions that her sister, a difficult person, is feeling so embarrassed and ashamed that she is afraid to be seen on the streets.

When the caseworker visits my mother, however, she finds her cheerful, poised, and seemingly very satisfied with her pregnancy, which she says she had not really expected, because she had been having partial periods until the fourth month. In no way does she seem ashamed or regretful. In fact, at one point, when the worker slips and refers to the baby as "him," my mother, according to the narrative, beams and tells the writer she has all along been looking forward to having a boy.

The worker asks my mother about the father of the baby. My mother says she is very much in love with him—but refuses to name him. She says she does not even want to tell him about her pregnancy for fear that he will give up his career to support her. The only reason she will even entertain the thought of an adoption is to keep the father out of it, something the worker says sounds unfair.

But then it becomes immediately clear that my mother is in no way willing to surrender her child. When she tentatively asks what an adoption would entail, she seems almost relieved to hear that she would be cut off entirely. There is no way, she says, that she will give her child up to a family she doesn't know and not be permitted to continue on as the child's mother, seeing him as often as she wants. Other alternatives are explored. My mother insists that, whatever arrangement is made—foster care or an orphanage—she will have to be able to visit her child and supervise his care. Foster care is settled on. For the first month of my life, I live with a foster family in White Plains. But then, when my mother complains that I am not doing well, I am sent to the orphanage. I knew none of this.

The report offers in copious detail the ins and outs of the family drama that ensued. All of the characters that I knew in my childhood and had retained in adult memory as mythical personae were here present, but in ways I had never seen before.

When I was finally placed in the Home for Hebrew Infants, complications ensued, twists and turns of plot and motive abounded. Lee insisted that records be fudged; my mother demanded that rules be altered so she could have additional visiting rights. Financial arrangements became murky. Though the family had no trouble meeting the fee of thirty dollars per month, it was difficult coming up with a signed guarantor, a state requirement. In the beginning, Morty agreed to do this—but he never followed through, finally acknowledging that he was worried about his reputation. And then there was the question of the ultimate disposition of the child: a child could not remain in the institution beyond the age of three.

The writer focused throughout on my mother. She follows her hopes, troubles, practical difficulties, uncertainties. The one constant—according to the writer—was my mother's determination to hold on to me. Her plan to do this was far-fetched but breathtaking in its simplicity. Her idea was to make all her relatives love me.

To do this, she first has to get everyone to visit the home. This is not so easily done. Initially, only my grandmother is willing. Harriet and Lee, who understand what my mother is up to perfectly, adamantly refuse. But eventually they come around, along with everyone else. Most of the report covers this unrelenting campaign of my mother's. When the family finally does give in and agrees to have me taken home as a foster child so that my grandfather, still in the dark, can also be wooed—and then told the truth—the writer notes, on November 18, 1936, "Worker met Miss Stone visiting at the HHI and was told by her rather gleefully that plans were on the way for taking David home."

My mother is magnanimous and generous in her victory. The writer observes, at one point, "Miss Stone did not express much resentment. She said her sister was a sweet person, but very much attached to conventions. Her aunt, too, was very straitlaced. Both, she knew, were interested in her and were trying to advise her for what they thought was her own benefit. Of course, she would not have preferred to have a child born out of wedlock but the fact remains that he had come, that he was her child, that she was attached to him and was not about to let him go."

I looked at the report again and again, into the heart of the secret that had finally been uncovered, and I realized how much I had missed. My mother lost friends, alienated her family, gave up her plans to be an actress, took any job that came along—stenotype operator, office clerk—to make sure she held on to her child. Her devotion to me was absolute.

And there was a simple corollary to this, one that stood out against all the troubles she endured: I was the child of the man she loved, the one whose name and reputation she refused to disclose.

When my mother was asked by the caseworker about the identity of the father, she resorted to storytelling. She first said the father was one of the last Jewish medical students in Nazi Germany. Then she admitted she had been lying, that the father was really a political activist. Pressed to name him, she would not. She protected the identity of the man she loved with all the ardor and devotion of Jane Eyre for the scourged and blasted Rochester.

My father, Van Heflin, was the love of her life.

Of course, nothing in the report says this. It is even clear from the narrative that my mother had been jilted. But this made no difference. She would not, could not bring herself to say a harsh word about her lover, even though it was clear he had abandoned her. Forty years later, when she finally got around to telling me about Van Heflin, she still would not do that. There was not a word—not the barest hint of anger or resentment in anything she said about him. But there were words from *Jane Eyre* that my mother put in her thesis:

> Do you think I can stay to become nothing to you? . . . If God had gifted me with some beauty, and much wealth, I should have made it as hard for you to leave me, as it is now for me to leave you. I am not talking to you now through the medium of custom, convention- alities, or even of mortal flesh: it is my spirit that addressed your spirit; just as if both had passed through the grave, and we stood at God's feet, equal,—as we are!

When I tried to envision that brief period in which my mother was happy with Van Heflin, I could not do it. I kept seeing her face as a drama-stricken mask on the lawn at Cla- verack, as a stony mask in the days when we were no longer talking, as a balloon when she drifted slowly out of this life. I tried to see her as she was then, a girl of eighteen, perhaps in her fantastic getup for the evening. What would it have been like to enter a room on a chilly November night, warmed by the buzz of the crowd, the sight of familiar faces? Perhaps her eyes caught his at a distant table, perhaps his caught hers. Maybe they were introduced later that night—or the next evening or the evening after that. They might have gone to parties together, taken walks through the streets, or ferry rides late at night, standing close to each other at the railing watching the city skyline and the dark-lit waste of the harbor, talking about their hopes, fears, their faces so close, their lips finally touching . . . the first kiss. . . . They read to each other. My mother gave him a book one day. It was an Irish fantasy about a young girl who is seduced by Pan but then falls in love with Angus Og, the god and protector of the clans, whose son she is going to carry. She is initiated into feeling unashamed of her own body, to exult in the wild flow of her energy. And then the protector of the clans allows her to see her own Divine Imagination. The two gods vie for her. She is asked by them what she believes in most. Happiness, she says, and understands in that moment that Angus Og, who weeps in the night for all the unhappiness he has seen, needs her more than anyone. In this union with him she understands that the knowledge of a man has to be joined to the gaiety of a child and that happiness itself is part of a mighty organism, larger than herself or him, large enough to banish unhappiness from the earth.

Why wouldn't she have wanted me to see that? The answer seems clear enough. She had her life to protect—the one she made with another man, a good man devoted to her and the family they made together. I had been raised in that family, had been its firstborn son. Why would she have wanted me to see anything else? I cannot enter that earlier time in my mother's life. It is a privileged place, one that she deliberately kept to herself but which, in the end, she gave up to me because I needed it for my life. She told me all I needed to know: I was a child of light and of happiness and nothing could ever change that or take it away.

ACKNOWLEDGMENTS

There are too many people to thank for help along the way. Thanks to my brother, Daniel, who has been there for me since our living-room B-17 days; thanks to Judy, to Harold Reis, to Harriet Bickart, and the late Morton Bickart. Thanks to all those who gave me their time, memories, and more: Ruth Fletcher, Florence Rossi, Max J. Rosenberg, Murray Nathan, Gus and Marie Tyler, Penny and Chana Melnick, Harold Goldstein, Ruth Levine, Maria Cardenal. Thanks to my friends Ricardo Nirenberg, Ina Campbell, and Esther Wanning, and all my friends at the Writer's Studio. For patience, belief, and hard work, thanks to David Black and Gary Morris at Black, Inc. To my children, Ellen, Ivan, and Maggie, I owe a special debt of gratitude, not only for their love and support but because they helped me with what I could not or would not see.

But I would never have finished this book without the active involvement of two people in every phase of the writing. To Jenny Dowling, my former wife of thirty-two years, and to my editor, Jon Segal, who has been a friend as well as the keenest and most sensitive of editors, I owe far more than I can ever acknowledge here.

A NOTE ABOUT THE AUTHOR

*David Siff lives in New York. Under the name
David Falkner, he has been an actor and, more recently,
a journalist and the author of a number
of books on sports.*

A NOTE ON THE TYPE

The text of this book was set in Weiss, a typeface designed in Germany by Emil Rudolf Weiss (1875–1942). The design of the roman was completed in 1928 and that of the italic in 1931. Both are well balanced and even in color, and both reflect the subtle skill of a fine calligrapher.

Composed by North Market Street Graphics, Lancaster, Pennsylvania

Printed and bound by Quebecor Printing, Martinsburg, West Virginia

Designed by Iris Weinstein